WILD HARVEST 2

WILD HARVEST 2

NICK NAIRN

Edited by Andrew Meehan

BBC BOOKS

FOR MUM

This book is published to accompany the television series entitled *Wild Harvest 2* which was first broadcast in 1997. The series was produced by Ideal World Limited for BBC Scotland.
Series Producer: Hamish Barbour
Director: Graham Strong

Published by BBC Books,
an imprint of BBC Worldwide Publishing,
BBC Worldwide Limited, Woodlands,
80 Wood Lane, London W12 0TT

First published 1997

ISBN 0 563 38318 6

Photographs by Graham Lees

Set in Spectrum, Felix and Gills Sans Condensed by Ace Filmsetting Limited, Frome
Printed in Great Britain by Cambus Litho Limited, East Kilbride
Bound in Great Britain by Hunter & Foulis Limited, Edinburgh
Colour separations by Radstock Reproductions Limited, Midsomer Norton
Jacket printed by Lawrence Allen Limited, Weston-super-Mare

CONTENTS

ACKNOWLEDGEMENTS

Thanks to Colin Cameron and Ken MacQuarrie for recommissioning *Wild Harvest*; Debbie Major for all her hard work in testing the recipes and keeping me sane; Graham Lees for his wonderful photographs; Graham Strong, Hamish Barbour and all the crew members for making *Wild Harvest 2* a cracking series; Barbara Levy for such professional sound advice; Khadija Manjlai for making it happen; and Nicky Copeland and the rest of the BBC Books team.

Above all, a huge thank you to the most fantastic staff at Braeval for helping me through a very busy year: head chef Dan Hall, sous-chef Jeremy Warres, commis-chef Sam Carter, manager Jean Bond, deputy manager Shona McLean, Louise, Chantal, Jenny, Ruth, Gillian and Jemma. And, of course, to Fiona for keeping it all together.

INTRODUCTION

Travelling around Scotland has reaffirmed my faith – as if I ever needed it – in the strength of the natural produce available to us these days. I've hand-dived my own scallops; been up all night in search of a sea trout, and got down on my hands and knees in the forest foraging for wild mushrooms. People say that we have no legacy of fine dining in this country, yet we have the finest raw ingredients in the world. Something, somewhere is amiss.

You can still walk into a restaurant half a mile from the shore and be offered the culinary equivalent of an Engelbert Humperdinck record: lurid orange breaded haddock with a geriatric lemon wedge. What is this? Where are we? How do they get away with it?

The good news is that some wise folks have refocused their efforts, and the best game, seafood, fruit and vegetables are finding their way to Scottish tables rather than the fast track to restaurants abroad. They tend to be tucked-out-of-the-way chef/proprietor restaurants with a commitment to finding and providing the best local and seasonal fare they can. Every town needs at least a couple of places like that – unassumingly friendly, comfortable, honest.

But not everyone can cook to restaurant standard – why should they? – and everyone has to start somewhere. My mother was a natural; three kids, one husband, and dinner on the table six nights a week at exactly six o'clock. I say natural because she effortlessly juggled a roast in the oven, constant comings and goings and an Aga going full throttle.

I was a natural at mixing gin and tonics, but the rest didn't fall into place until much, much later. The thing was, I *liked* hanging out in the kitchen, but the aspiration to become a good cook was fuelled by something else entirely. I was home on leave from the Navy and Man does not live on canned spaghetti sauce alone. A crash course on how to get cooking without getting burned soon followed. My biggest brainstorm was to serve up chicken stuffed with hazelnuts and grapes. The reviews were not good.

Then I learned to loosen up, and realised there was no big mystery: it's just food, the simpler the better. With a good sharp knife and a chopping board, you're really halfway there. Time passes and tastes change, but I've included one of those early dishes here: Pot-roast Chicken Paprika (see page 94) – the proverbial crowd-pleaser and a veritable one-dish wonder. Chop everything up, throw it in the pot and it cooks itself.

You'll also notice I've included childhood throwbacks such as Garlic Mushrooms on Toast (see page 40) and Lemon and Sugar Crêpes (see page 165). They don't have to aspire to anything fancy as they sit elbow-to-elbow with much more complex dishes – different ideas for different moods. Just try something you know will hit the target.

Anyone who has watched *Wild Harvest* may think I'm obsessed with setting the dinner on fire, but not everything has to be a full-blown, pin-back-the-curtains-and-call-the-fire-brigade job. I *do* believe in sealing in flavours quickly and doing as little as possible to food on its journey to the plate, but I've included a few warming roasts and stews for those of you who live in the same frozen part of the world as me. So, what page would I turn to first? Have a glass of wine and watch *Eat Drink Man Woman* on video. Then you can slurp some hearty Scotch Broth (page 20), poke around aromatic Goat's Cheese Soufflés (page 42), flake off chunks of the simplest seared sea bass (page 22), slice into a glistening fillet of beef (page 111), toy with a home-made Cherry and Almond Tart (page 157), and remember that you have the best food in the world on your doorstep. Enjoy.

SPECIAL EQUIPMENT

Here is a list of some kitchen equipment which will actively help your cooking ambitions, rather than clutter up your kitchen drawers:

FRYING PANS: The best to use are black iron. They are all metal, which means that they can be put straight into the oven. They need to be seasoned prior to use (not unlike a wok) and are superb for cooking with. Also, they're cheap and last forever.

MANDOLIN GRATER: Not essential, but very useful for larger quantities of slicing and grating. It has the added advantage of being millimetre-accurate for fine slicing. The plastic Japanese ones are very sharp, cheap and, if you're not careful, sore on your fingers. You have been warned.

CHINOIS SIEVE: A fine-mesh, conical metal sieve. Very handy for straining stocks and sauces.

PASTA MACHINE: Indispensable for fresh pasta.

SCONE CUTTERS: Buy the heaviest and strongest you can find. They are useful for cutting out Dauphinoise potatoes, shaping fishcakes, salmon tartares and many other things – including scones, I suppose.

HAND-HELD BLENDER: Or 'stick liquidiser'. These small electric liquidisers have revolutionised sauce making, allowing anyone to make light, frothy sauces and banishing 'split' sauces to the past.

KILNER JARS: These swing top jars with replaceable rubber seals are handy for storing Pesto, Tapenade, Home-Dried Tomatoes and practically anything else you can cram them with. Give them a good old wash before use and ensure that anything kept in them is covered in olive oil.

KNIVES: A large chef's knife (I use a 30 cm/12 in knife) and a flexible boning knife, combined with a good chopping board and a sharpening steel, will aid your cooking no end.

Other useful implements are a good-quality lemon zester and a canelle cutter.

Getting good quality gear means saving time and effort on the day, so it is worth treating yourself – even if it's in instalments.

SEASONING: A wee word on seasoning. In the following recipes, you'll see that Maldon salt is almost ubiquitous. It's not as coarse as sea salt and better by far than regular salt. (The Men from Maldon haven't given me a bung for this, by the way, it has quite simply become an essential ingredient of my cooking.) I hardly ever use black pepper, as I find the flavour very invasive, so I mainly use fresh-ground white pepper.

PART ONE

SOUPS

SOUPS – AN INTRODUCTION

I love soup. I find it a very comforting thing, both to make and eat. Especially with slices of freshly baked bread slathered with good, unsalted butter. My own soups seldom have stock in them. I rely on good technique to get the best flavours from the ingredients.

BASIC SOUP RULES:

1) Use a ratio of approximately 25% onion to the main vegetable ingredient.
2) Cut the vegetables into the smallest pieces practicable – a 5 mm ($^1/_4$ in) dice. This reduces cooking time. (An electric food slicer is a handy thing for this.)
3) Always add *boiling* water to the vegetables as this reduces the time that the soup is off the boil, during which it can 'stew' and lose its freshness.
4) Once cooked, liquidise the soup and cool it as quickly as possible – this keeps its quality and flavour.
5) It's much easier to make a big batch of soup. That way you can

freeze it in handy-sized portions and then reliquidise it once defrosted and re-heated.

6) The soup is cooked once the vegetables are soft and tender. Timing varies for different vegetables.

APPROXIMATE COOKING TIME FOR VEGETABLES:

Artichoke: 35 minutes.
Broccoli: 10 minutes.
Carrot: 45 minutes.
Cauliflower: 45 minutes.
Mushroom: 40 minutes.
Parsnip: 50 minutes.
Pea: 3 minutes.
Spinach: 5 minutes.
Tomato: 20 minutes.
Watercress: 2 minutes.

CELERY AND TOMATO SOUP

A grand fresh soup which is nice to eat at any time of year but best in the summer when you can get really good ripe tomatoes. I use vine tomatoes for this – in other words, tomatoes picked when they are ripe and red that actually taste and smell of tomato. Even canned plum tomatoes are preferable to artificially ripened Dutch waterballs.

120 ml (4 fl oz) olive oil
225 g (8 oz) onions, finely sliced
1 garlic clove, crushed
450 g (1 lb) celery, finely sliced
750 g (1 1/2 lb) ripe tomatoes, roughly chopped
900 ml (1 1/2 pints) boiling water
Deep-fried Celery Leaves (see page 131), optional
Maldon salt
Freshly ground white pepper

SERVES SIX TO EIGHT

Warm the olive oil in a large saucepan and gently sweat the onions, garlic and celery until soft, probably about 10 minutes. Then add the tomatoes and some salt and pepper and cook for another 10 minutes, until the liquid from the tomatoes has evaporated. Add the boiling water, cover and simmer for 35 minutes, until the celery is nice and tender. Now liquidise the soup and pass it through a conical strainer or a fine sieve. Heat through gently. Don't forget to check the seasoning, and then dust it with the chives before you serve or pile on the deep-fried celery leaves. If you don't use it all at once, this soup freezes exceptionally well.

Potato and Parsley Soup with Truffle Oil

Soup is the ultimate liquid lunch and, with the addition of some prized truffle oil, this is your ultimate soup. The oil lends its special earthy flavours but the soup will still be great without it. To make it extra special you must add the cream and parsley at the last minute, then give it a good old thrash about with a hand blender to make it really light and frothy.

100 g (4 oz) butter
275 g (10 oz) onions, finely sliced
1 kg (2¼ lb) King Edward or Maris Piper potatoes, peeled and thinly sliced
1.2 litres (2 pints) boiling water
20 g (¾ oz) fresh flatleaf parsley, chopped, plus extra to garnish
85 ml (3 fl oz) double cream, lightly whipped
8 teaspoons truffle oil, to serve
Maldon salt
Freshly ground white pepper

SERVES EIGHT

Melt the butter in a large saucepan, add the onions and cook gently for about 5 minutes, until softened. Add the sliced potatoes and cook for about 2 minutes, then stir in some seasoning, say, 1 teaspoon of salt, and the boiling water. Bring back to the boil and skim any froth from the surface. Cover and simmer for 40 minutes, by which time the potatoes should be falling to bits. Purée the soup in a liquidiser and then pass it through a conical strainer or a fine sieve. Reheat gently, check the seasoning and adjust if necessary.

To serve, add the parsley and whipped cream and work with a hand blender until nice and frothy (or simply whizz everything together in a liquidiser). Pour into heated bowls, drizzle with the sensuously rich truffle oil and a little more parsley. This soup freezes well without the cream.

OVERLEAF:
Left: Celery and Tomato Soup (see opposite)
Right: Potato and Parsley Soup with Truffle Oil (see above)

Spicy Chick Pea and Chorizo Soup

The warm, spicy flavour of chorizo sausages can be used in many different ways. I particularly like them with pulses and rice. However, there are few worse things than undercooked pulses, so make sure you soak the chick peas overnight in plenty of water. They can take forever to cook but if you can crush one between your thumb and forefinger, it's ready. Keep cooking if they're still crunchy, in order to avoid a lumpy porridge. This soup also freezes well.

175 g (6 oz) dried chick peas
225 g (8 oz) onions, finely sliced
1 celery stick, finely chopped
1 leek, finely chopped
2 garlic cloves, crushed
85 ml (3 fl oz) olive oil
1 tablespoon Chilli Oil (see page 175)
1 teaspoon curry paste
1 teaspoon tomato purée
400 g (14 oz) can of tomatoes
100 g (4 oz) chorizo sausage, finely diced
1.2 litres (2 pints) boiling water
1 tablespoon chopped fresh basil or chives
Maldon salt
Freshly ground white pepper
Olive oil, to serve

SERVES EIGHT

Cover the dried chick peas with plenty of cold water and leave to soak overnight.

The next day, sweat the onions, celery, leek and garlic in the olive oil until soft. Stir in the chilli oil and curry paste and some seasoning and cook for 3–4 minutes. Add the tomato purée and canned tomatoes and bring to a simmer. Then it's time to add the drained chick peas and diced chorizo. Pour in the boiling water, cover and simmer for 1½–3 hours, depending on the chick peas. You may have to top the soup up with a bit more water. When the chick peas are tender, you can either liquidise the mixture or, if you like a nice textured soup, serve it as it is. But don't forget to check the seasoning and garnish with the fresh basil or chives. A little olive oil drizzled over each bowlful just before serving is also nice.

Pea, apple and curry soup

This is the most surprising combination of flavours I have tried this year. Unlikely-sounding but very tasty. The sweetness of the peas is offset by the mild acidity and fruitiness of the apples. The curry deepens the flavours and adds a spicy note, but shouldn't dominate.

Melt the butter in a large saucepan and add the onions, garlic, ginger, curry paste and a little seasoning. Cook gently for 8–10 minutes, until softened, then add the apples and cook for a further 4 minutes. Stir in the peas and boiling water, bring to the boil, cover and simmer for 5 minutes. Now purée in a liquidiser, then pass through a conical strainer or a fine sieve. Heat through gently and adjust the seasoning. Serve immediately, with a good blob of crème fraîche. This soup freezes well.

75 g (3 oz) unsalted butter
175 g (6 oz) onions, thinly sliced
2 garlic cloves, crushed
2 cm (3/4 in) piece of root ginger, crushed
1 tablespoon mild curry paste
3 Granny Smith apples, cored and grated but not peeled
275 g (10 oz) good-quality frozen peas
1.2 litres (2 pints) boiling water
Maldon salt
Freshly ground white pepper
Crème fraîche, to serve

SERVES SIX

Celeriac and leek soup

If truth be told, this recipe was stolen from my long-suffering sous chef, Dan Hall. He snuck it onto the menu at Braeval one night and the combination of flavours knocked me out. It's hard to say where it originally came from. Nevertheless, this soup is too good not to share with you.

100 g (4 oz) butter
225 g (8 oz) onions, finely chopped
450 g (1 lb) leeks, finely sliced
450 g (1 lb) celeriac, peeled and grated
225 g (8 oz) potatoes, peeled and finely sliced
1.75 litres (3 pints) boiling water
150 ml (5 fl oz) double cream, lightly whipped
1 tablespoon chopped fresh chives
Maldon salt
Freshly ground white pepper

SERVES EIGHT TO TEN

Melt the butter in a large saucepan and sweat the onions and leeks until soft. Add the celeriac and potatoes and some seasoning. Remember to give it a stir to make sure everything is well coated, then pour on the boiling water. Bring it all to a simmer, cover and cook for 45 minutes, until the vegetables are tender. Liquidise the soup, pass it through a conical strainer or a fine sieve, then reheat gently and check the seasoning.

To serve, add the lightly whipped cream and give it a good thrash about with an electric hand blender till it's nice and frothy. Check the seasoning again and pour into bowls, then garnish with the chives. This soup freezes well without the cream.

Salt cod soup with black olives

I love salt cod so much that I couldn't resist including this recipe. You could use smoked haddock if you can't get salt cod but there will be a big change in flavour. The olives, too, could go, so you'll end up in a roundabout fashion with that traditional Scottish soup, cullen skink.

450 g (1 lb) salt cod
1.2 litres (2 pints) milk
300 ml (10 fl oz) double cream
300 ml (10 fl oz) olive oil
225 g (8 oz) onions, thinly sliced
4 garlic cloves, crushed
450 g (1 lb) potatoes, such as Maris Piper, peeled and thinly sliced
28 black olives, stoned and finely diced
1 tablespoon finely chopped fresh chives
Olive Oil Croûtons (see page 184)
Freshly ground white pepper

SERVES SIX TO EIGHT

Soak the salt cod for 24 hours in at least 4 changes of water, then drain.

Bring the milk and cream to the boil in a large saucepan, add the salt cod and bring back to the boil. Remove from the heat, cover and leave for about 5 minutes, by which time the cod should be almost cooked.

Heat almost all the olive oil in a separate pan and sweat the onions and garlic until nicely softened. Add the potatoes and stir to coat them in the oil. Cook for about 5 minutes, adding a little freshly ground white pepper. You won't need any salt because the cod is pretty salty.

Strain the milk and cream over the potatoes and onions and bring to the boil. Cover and simmer for 35 minutes. While you are doing this, keep the cod covered with a butter wrapper or some buttered greaseproof paper to prevent it drying out. It's fine to leave it in the pan.

When the potatoes are soft and falling apart, add the cod and bring the mixture back to a simmer. Now liquidise the soup and pass it through a conical strainer or a fine sieve. Reheat gently and check the seasoning. If the soup is too thick it can be thinned with some more milk.

To serve, pour the soup into heated serving bowls and scatter over a generous amount of finely diced black olives, a dusting of chives and a little drizzle of the remaining olive oil. Finally, after all that, throw on a few olive oil croûtons and enjoy. This soup shouldn't be frozen.

My scotch broth

I've been reasonably faithful to this, a soup most Scots were brought up on, though I've replaced the traditional lamb with beef and left out the split peas. It's as if the Nineties had never happened.

450 g (1 lb) shin of beef
1.2 litres (2 pints) cold water
40 g (1 1/2 oz) pearl barley
1 potato, cut into 5 mm (1/4 in) dice
1 carrot, cut into 5 mm (1/4 in) dice
1 celery stick, cut into 5 mm (1/4 in) dice
1 onion, cut into 5 mm (1/4 in) dice
1 leek, cut into 5 mm (1/4 in) dice
2 tablespoons chopped fresh parsley
Maldon salt
Freshly ground white pepper

SERVES FOUR

Put the shin of beef and the water into a large pan. Add some seasoning, bring to the boil, then cover and simmer very slowly for about 1 1/2 hours, until the meat is very tender. Lift the meat out onto a plate and set aside to cool slightly.

Put the pearl barley in the pan, bring back to the boil and simmer for 10 minutes. Add the potato and simmer for 10 minutes. Then add the carrot, celery, onion and leek and simmer for a further 15 minutes. If at this stage the soup looks a bit too thick, add a little more water and bring back to a simmer.

Cut the cooked shin of beef into 5 mm (1/4 in) dice and add to the soup with the chopped parsley. Check the seasoning and serve – it tastes even better if it's left to cool and then reheated the next day. It also freezes well.

PART TWO

FISH STARTERS

FISH – AN INTRODUCTION

Buying a ready-filleted fish is always a bit of a gamble, since you never know how fresh the thing is. Always try to get a fishmonger to fillet a whole fish for you. It is his job, after all. That aside, not only is fish very good for you, it is also an exciting and rewarding raw ingredient, offering flavour and variety.

When buying fish, look out for the following:

- Bright, prominent eyes – not dull and sunken.
- Pink gills with no trace of brown.
- Should have a clear, odourless slime on skin – no dryness.
- Flesh should be firm, not flabby.
- Should have a clean sea odour – shouldn't smell 'fishy'.
- No bruising on the flesh.

Shellfish should be bought alive. If this is not possible, look out for these tell-tale signs: fresh shellfish have a clean smell, not a strong odour. With mussels and scallops, the fresh fish have tightly closed shells.

Now let's get on with it.

Seared sea bass, chilli and bok choy stir-fry with a lime and coriander juice

It's worth going to the effort of getting sea bass, which probably has the best flavour of any white-fleshed fish. Get your fishmonger to scale and fillet it. Two 450 g (1 lb) fish will give 4 starter-sized portions, but will probably cost you £12. If this sounds a bit much, fresh Scottish farmed salmon can be used instead. Bok choy is available from Chinese supermarkets and is a bit like a chunky lettuce. It only needs a minimum of cooking and that has to be done at the last minute. You'll need at least 2 frying pans. The sauce is very low in calories and so is very healthy.

25 g (1 oz) leek, finely diced
25 g (1 oz) carrot, finely diced
25 g (1 oz) fennel, finely diced
4 tablespoons olive oil
250 ml (8 fl oz) Nage (see page 168)
4 tablespoons sunflower oil
4 sea bass fillets, skin on
275 g (10 oz) bok choy, roughly chopped
2 tablespoons Thai fish sauce (*nam pla*)
Juice and zest of 1 lime
2 tablespoons chopped fresh coriander
1 red chilli, finely diced
Maldon salt
Freshly ground white pepper

SERVES FOUR

First make the sauce base. Sweat the leek, carrot and fennel in 2 tablespoons of the olive oil for 2–3 minutes. Add the nage and bring to the boil, then remove from the heat and set aside.

You can cook the bok choy and the bass simultaneously, so heat 2 frying pans and add 2 tablespoons of sunflower oil to each one. Put the bass fillets skin-side down in one pan and the bok choy in the other. Stir-fry the leaves until wilted, then add 1 tablespoon of the Thai fish sauce, 1 teaspoon of the lime juice and some seasoning. Turn the fish fillets after 3–4 minutes. The skin should be crisp. Cook the other side for 1 minute only, then lift the fish out of the pan and season with salt and pepper. Tip the bok choy into a bowl. If this all sounds a bit frenetic, the bok choy can be cooked first and kept in a bowl.

To serve, heat through the sauce base, then add the coriander, the remaining fish sauce and lime juice, lime zest, chilli and the remaining olive oil. Place a mound of bok choy in the middle of each shallow bowl and spoon the juice around. The bass fillet goes on top and you're ready to go.

SALMON CARPACCIO, CARPACCIO SAUCE

There's no better place to eat carpaccio – a simple classic of very thinly sliced raw beef with sauce drizzled over it – than Harry's Bar in Venice. I thought it was magnificent and tried it using salmon – splendid. Make sure the salmon is really fresh and that you've got a razor-sharp knife. You can make up the plates in advance, cover them in clingfilm and keep in the fridge until you're ready to serve.

Use the middle cut from a salmon fillet, skinned and boned, and slice it finely at a 45 degree angle. It helps to wrap the fillet in clingfilm and put in the freezer for 15 minutes – no longer – then unwrap and slice.

175 g (6 oz) raw salmon, thinly sliced

FOR THE SAUCE:

4 tablespoons mayonnaise
5 tablespoons single cream
2 teaspoons mustard
1–2 teaspoons lemon juice

TO SERVE:

1 tablespoon chopped fresh dill
Maldon salt
Freshly ground white pepper

SERVES FOUR

You can make the sauce up to 12 hours in advance. Mix the mayonnaise, cream, mustard and lemon juice together, put them in a plastic sauce bottle or a small bowl and keep in the fridge.

Lay the slices of raw salmon on large plates, arranging them so that they cover the whole surface. Drizzle with the sauce, season well, scatter with the chopped dill and there you have it – a salmon carpaccio that would make a Venetian proud.

Seared Salmon with Potato Pancakes and Spring Onion Crème Fraîche

This is just one use for these delicious potato pancakes – the warm pancake, the barely cooked salmon with its crisp coating, crunchy spring onions and melting crème fraîche. Ask the fishmonger for 5 mm ($^1/_4$ in) thick slices, around 75 g (3 oz) in weight, of salmon cut from a whole side.

FOR THE PANCAKE:

350 g (12 oz) floury potatoes
2 tablespoons plain flour
2–3 tablespoons milk
2 tablespoons double cream
2 medium eggs
2 tablespoons sunflower oil

FOR THE CRÈME FRAîCHE:

4 spring onions, finely chopped
100 g (4 oz) crème fraîche
1 teaspoon lemon juice
A few drops of Tabasco sauce

FOR THE SALMON:

1–2 tablespoons sunflower oil
4 thin slices of salmon
Maldon salt
Freshly ground white pepper

TO SERVE:

Salad of Herbs (see page 131)
1 spring onion, cut in strips and curled in iced water
Herb Oil (see page 176)

SERVES FOUR

Pre-heat the oven to 240°C/475°F/Gas Mark 9.

Peel the potatoes and cook them in boiling salted water until tender, then drain well and mash. Beat in the flour with a wooden spoon, add the milk and cream and mix well. Beat in the eggs, season and work it all through a sieve to remove any lumps.

Heat the sunflower oil in a 20 cm (8 in) ovenproof frying pan until hot and then pour in the pancake mixture. It should be about 1 cm ($^1/_2$ in) thick. As soon as it starts to bubble and brown around the edges, put the frying pan into the top of the hot oven and leave for 10 minutes. Alternatively, make 4 individual round pancakes in an 11.5 cm (4 ½ cm) blini pan and grill them to finish.

Meanwhile, make the spring onion crème fraîche by mixing together the spring onions, crème fraîche, lemon juice, Tabasco and seasoning. Remove the pancake from the oven using a strong pair of oven gloves. It should be well risen and lightly browned on top, and will keep in a warm place for 20–30 minutes.

Heat a large frying pan until very hot. Add the sunflower oil and flash-fry the salmon on one side only for about 2 minutes. Transfer to a baking sheet and season on the cooked side only.

To serve, quarter the pancake and place on 4 warmed plates. Put a piece of seared salmon on each pancake and on top of that goes a good spoonful of the crème fraîche. Top with salad, scatter onion curls round the edge of the plate and drizzle with herb oil.

Langoustine Salad with Hot Garlic Butter, Parsley and Lemon Dressing

There's no doubt that langoustines are the finest prawns you can get – but freshness is *so* important. If you are cooking them yourself, you should buy live ones, with that beautiful deep orange colour and translucent glow. Dead langoustines turn a dull yellow and release an enzyme that breaks down the flesh in the tail, turning it into cotton wool. If you don't want to cook them, buy them precooked from a fishmonger you can trust. Good-quality large cooked fresh prawns are a good substitute.

900 g (2 lb) live langoustines or 225 g (8 oz) cooked and peeled fresh prawns
50 g (2 oz) fresh peas or mangetout (optional)
100 g (4 oz) unsalted butter
1 large garlic clove (or more if you like), well crushed
2 tablespoons lemon juice
Finely grated zest of ½ lemon
150 g (5 oz) mixed salad leaves
2 plum Tomatoes Concassées (see page 181)
1 tablespoon chopped fresh parsley
Maldon salt
Freshly ground white pepper

SERVES FOUR

If you are using live langoustines, have a large pot of boiling water ready on a fierce heat. Drop in the whole langoustines, bring back to the boil and cook for 2 minutes. With a slotted spoon, transfer them straight to a big bowl of iced water to stop the cooking process. Let them cool and then pull off the tails. Crack the shells and just ease out the meat.

Blanch the peas or mangetout, if using, in boiling water for about 1 minute, just to set the colour and soften them slightly. Drain, refresh in cold water and set aside.

Make the dressing. Gently melt the butter with the garlic and lemon zest. Cook very slowly for 3 minutes to take some of the harshness from the garlic, then add the lemon juice and a little seasoning. Set aside.

Tear the salad leaves to a manageable size if necessary and put them in a bowl with the peas or mangetout. Season and mix well, then pile up in the centre of 4 serving plates.

To serve, heat the dressing until just boiling. Add the parsley, the langoustines or prawns and the tomatoes and mix well. Spoon some of the dressing over the salad and the shellfish and the rest of the dressing around the edge of the plates.

Roast Scallops with Couscous and a Rich Shellfish Sauce

Scallops are sweet and succulent and lend themselves to the neatest of presentations. The scallops Alan Peace provided for the filming of *Wild Harvest* were delicious and plump, and so fresh that they almost crunch in the mouth. The tomato liquid I use as a basis for the sauce is superb but you can substitute vegetable stock. The beautiful orange corals from the scallops add more colour and flavour to the sauce, while the couscous soaks it all up nicely.

225 g (8 oz) fresh, ripe plum tomatoes, cut into quarters
A few fresh basil leaves
A few fresh tarragon leaves
8 nice large fresh scallops, with their corals, shelled
275 ml (9 fl oz) Nage (see page 168) or Fish Stock (see page 169)
175 g (6 oz) couscous
4 spring onions, finely chopped
2 red chillies, seeded and finely chopped
2 tablespoons Japanese pickled ginger, finely chopped

PREVIOUS PAGES:
Left: Seared Salmon with Potato Pancakes and Spring Onion Crème Fraîche (see page 24)
Right: Langoustine Salad with Hot Garlic Butter, Parsley and Lemon Dressing (see page 25)

The day before, put the tomatoes in a food processor with the basil and tarragon leaves and some salt and pepper. Process for a few seconds until coarsely chopped but be careful not to purée them. Tip them into a muslin-lined sieve set over a large mixing bowl and leave to drain overnight in the fridge or somewhere cool. The following day you will have about 85 ml (3 fl oz) of light-coloured but intensely flavoured tomato juice as the base for the shellfish sauce. Time-consuming but well worth it.

Detach the corals from the scallops, cut them into small dice and set aside for the sauce. Cut each scallop horizontally into 3 or 4 discs and set aside.

Bring the nage or fish stock to the boil in a large pan. Then add the couscous in a slow, steady stream, stirring all the time. It should end up looking like a thick porridge. Remove from the heat, cover with a tight-fitting lid and leave for 5 minutes to allow the mixture to swell nicely. Then fluff up the grains with a fork and add the chopped spring onions, chillies, pickled ginger, coriander, mint, garlic and lime zest. Add 1 tablespoon of the lime juice, olive oil and seasoning. Cover and set aside – it can be reheated after it has cooled, if you wish.

For the shellfish sauce, put the tomato juice into a small pan and bring to the boil. Add the diced scallop corals and either give the mixture a good old thrash with a hand blender or tip it into a liqidiser, blend until smooth and then return to the pan. Now add the cold diced butter, either by whisking in a few pieces at a time over a low heat or giving it another whizz with the hand blender. Adjust the seasoning and keep warm, but don't let it boil.

Heat a frying pan over a high heat. Add the clarified butter or sunflower oil and the scallop slices and cook for about 1 minute on just one side. Quickly transfer to a baking tray, cooked-side up, season with salt and pepper and sprinkle with a little of the remaining lime juice.

To serve, put a large scone cutter on each plate, pack in the couscous and remove the cutter (this gives a neat shape). Pour the sauce around and arrange the scallop slices on top of the couscous.

- 2 tablespoons chopped fresh coriander
- 1 tablespoon chopped fresh mint
- 1 garlic clove, crushed
- Juice and finely grated zest of 1 lime
- 3 tablespoons olive oil
- 50 g (2 oz) cold unsalted butter, diced
- 1 tablespoon Clarified Butter (see page 184) or sunflower oil
- Maldon salt
- Freshly ground white pepper

SERVES FOUR

SQUID TEMPURA WITH LEMON RICE AND CHILLI OIL

I first tried this combination on the television programme *Ready Steady Cook*. I was under pressure and 4 million people were watching but it worked. I love the tender squid in the crisp batter, without a hint of greasiness (see page 66). Try to get small squid and persuade your fishmonger to clean them for you. The rice can be cooked in advance and reheated, and the chilli oil also benefits from being made in advance. This leaves you free to concentrate on cooking the squid, which needs to be done at the last moment.

First make the lemon rice. Put the rice into a pan and cover with water, then add 1/2 teaspoon of salt and bring to the boil. Simmer for 15 minutes, until just tender, then pour into a large sieve set over a bowl. Leave until well drained. Next, heat a large frying pan or wok until very hot. Add the sunflower oil and stir-fry the bacon in it until crisp. Now add the rice and the peas and stir-fry for another 3 minutes. Then mix

- 225 g (8 oz) cleaned squid
- Lemon juice
- Maldon salt
- Freshly ground white pepper
- Sunflower oil for deep-frying
- 4 tablespoons Chilli Oil (see page 175)

Sprigs of fresh coriander, to garnish (optional)

FOR THE LEMON RICE:

225 g (8 oz) long grain rice
2 tablespoons sunflower oil
3 smoked streaky bacon rashers, rinded and chopped
75 g (3 oz) frozen peas, thawed
Juice and finely grated zest of 1 lemon
1 tablespoon finely chopped fresh chives

FOR THE BATTER:

100 g (4 oz) plain flour
50 g (2 oz) cornflour
175 ml (6 fl oz) cold water
1 egg yolk
2 egg whites

SERVES FOUR

in the lemon juice and zest and the chives. Keep warm. If you are preparing the rice in advance, you can leave the chives until the last minute and reheat the rice in the microwave or oven.

Slice the squid into thin rings and separate the tentacles if large. Season with a little lemon juice and salt and pepper and set aside.

For the batter, mix the flour, cornflour, water and egg yolk in a bowl with some seasoning. In a separate bowl, whisk the egg whites until they form soft peaks and then fold them into the batter. This can be kept for up to 30 minutes but is best used straight away.

Pour the oil for deep-frying into a pan until it is one-third full and heat it to 190°C/375°F. Dip the pieces of squid in the batter and fry a few at a time for about 2 minutes, until crisp and golden. You may need to turn the pieces half way through cooking, so don't overcrowd the pan. Drain the squid on kitchen paper and keep warm while you cook the rest.

To serve, divide the rice between 4 warm serving plates. Place the squid pieces on top and drizzle the chilli oil round the outside. A sprig of coriander would work well as a garnish.

WARM SALAD OF NEW POTATOES AND SEARED TUNA WITH A NIÇOISE DRESSING

This is a reworking of the classic salad Niçoise, and one of the best things I've eaten this year. The fresh tuna must be in prime condition. The best part comes from the belly, which is nice and fatty and moister than the rest. Buy the best new potatoes you can. French pink Rosevals are perfect if available.

Scrub the potatoes and cook them in boiling salted water for 20 minutes or until tender. Drain, leave to cool and then cut lengthways into quarters. Cook the green beans in boiling salted water for 3 minutes, then drain and refresh under cold running water.

Prepare the dressing next. Put the shallots and olive oil in a small pan and warm through for 7–8 minutes, until the shallots have softened. Meanwhile, boil the egg for 8 minutes. Drain, leave until cold, then peel and cut into small dice. Add the olives, whole capers, anchovies and lemon juice to the pan with the olive oil and shallots. If you're doing this in advance, stop here. If you're serving straight away, add the tomatoes, diced egg and basil. Season with salt and pepper and keep warm.

To cook the fish, heat a frying pan until it is very hot. I use a ribbed cast iron pan which gives a nice stripy appearance to the steaks. Splash in the sunflower oil, then add the tuna steaks and cook for about 1½–2 minutes on either side, until well browned on the outside but nice and pink (not raw) inside. Remove from the pan, season on both sides with a little salt and pepper and set to one side.

Put the potato quarters, beans and curly endive into a bowl and add the olive oil, lemon juice and some seasoning. Toss to coat all the ingredients lightly. Divide the salad between 4 large plates, piling it as high as possible. Warm through the dressing, spoon it over and around the salad and place a tuna steak on top of each one.

450 g (1 lb) new potatoes
75 g (3 oz) fine green beans, halved
2 tablespoons sunflower oil
4 fresh tuna steaks, weighing about 75 g (3 oz) each
Leaves from the centre of 1 curly endive lettuce
1 tablespoon olive oil
1 teaspoon lemon juice
Maldon salt
Freshly ground white pepper

FOR THE NIÇOISE DRESSING:

2 shallots, finely diced
150 ml (5 fl oz) olive oil
1 large egg
12 black olives, stoned and finely diced
20 salted capers, rinsed and drained
8 anchovy fillets, drained and finely diced
2 tablespoons lemon juice
2 ripe plum Tomatoes Concassées (see page 181)
15 g (½ oz) fresh basil, finely chopped

SERVES FOUR

WARM SMOKED EEL AND APPLE TARTLETS WITH CIDER DRESSING

These tartlets provide a nice contrast in temperatures and textures – freshly cooked eel with crisp apples, tossed in a warm dressing and piled high into crisp, buttery pastry cases. Quickly pan-frying the eel intensifies the flavour and the smell, and the finished dish takes on an almost sweet and sour flavour which works really well. If you can't get hold of smoked eel, hot or cold smoked salmon could be used instead.

1 quantity Savoury Flan Pastry (see page 185)
2 Granny Smith apples
1 teaspoon lemon juice
1 frisée (or curly endive) lettuce
20 g (3/4 oz) flatleaf parsley
20 g (3/4 oz) chives
Sunflower oil for frying
100 g (4 oz) smoked eel fillets

FOR THE DRESSING:
300 ml (10 fl oz) sweet cider
3 tablespoons cider vinegar
135 ml (4 fl oz) olive oil
Maldon salt
Freshly ground white pepper
Balsamic Reduction (see page 178), to serve

SERVES FOUR

Pre-heat the oven to 200°C/400°F/Gas Mark 6.

Roll out the pastry on a lightly floured surface and use to line four 10 cm (4 in) tartlet cases. Bake blind as on page 185. Remove from the oven and leave to cool.

Press a melon baller deep into the surface of one apple and then twist to remove the flesh in balls. Continue over the surface of both apples. Add in the lemon juice and set aside in a large bowl.

Break the lettuce into small pieces, discarding most of the tough, dark green leaves. Break the parsley into sprigs, discarding any large stalks, and cut the chives in half, if very long. Add to the bowl with the apples.

For the dressing, put the cider into a pan and boil vigorously until reduced to a sticky liquid. Add the vinegar, oil and seasoning and whisk. Set aside.

Heat a frying pan until very hot. Add a thin film of oil, then the eel and fry for just 30 seconds on one side only. Remove to a plate.

To serve, add 2 tablespoons of the dressng to the apples and salad leaves and toss together gently. Pile evenly into the tartlet cases and then poke in pieces of the eel, tryng not to flatten the leaves too much. Lift onto 4 plates and spoon the rest of the dressing around the outside of each tartlet. Drizzle a little of the balsamic reduction around the edge of the plate, so that it mingles a little with the dressing.

PART THREE

OTHER STARTERS

TERRINE OF DUCK AND PORK WITH A SPICY PEAR CHUTNEY

There's no denying that a terrine involves plenty of advance preparation, but the up side is that it is easy to serve. Duck breast, or *magret*, is now available in most supermarkets. The larger male breasts are best for this recipe. The chutney benefits from being made a week or so in advance and will keep in a preserving jar for up to 3 months. The best terrine mould to use is a 1.2 litre (2-pint) Le Creuset terrine. You could use a 1 kg (2 lb) loaf tin but the terrine doesn't cook quite so evenly.

4 duck breasts, weighing about 275 g (10 oz) each
450 g (1 lb) pork belly, rind removed and roughly diced
25 g (1 oz) butter
4 shallots, finely chopped
2 garlic cloves, crushed
1 large sprig of fresh thyme
1 tablespoon green peppercorns in brine, drained
150 ml (5 fl oz) port
300 ml (10 fl oz) game or Chicken Stock (see page 170)
75 g (3 oz) pistachio nuts
1 egg
3 tablespoons chopped fresh flatleaf parsley
175 g (6 oz) rindless streaky bacon, very thinly sliced
5 bay leaves
Maldon salt
Freshly ground white pepper

First make the chutney. Melt the butter in a large saucepan and gently fry the onion, ginger and garlic with the mixed spice. When they are soft, add the tomato purée and Worcestershire sauce and cook for 1 minute. Now add the vinegar and sugar and bring to the boil. Next add the pears, sultanas and raisins and simmer for 25–30 minutes, until thickened. Check the seasoning and leave to cool. Put the chutney into a sterilised preserving jar and seal.

For the terrine, first skin the duck breasts with a sharp knife (keep the skin) and then cut 3 of them lengthwise into 6 strips each and set aside. Now roughly chop the other duck breast and pass it through a medium mincer blade together with the diced pork belly and the skin from the duck. Or take them along to your butcher and ask nicely.

Melt the butter in a frying pan, add the shallots and garlic and cook gently until softened. Increase the heat and add the leaves from the thyme sprig and the green peppercorns, and then the port. Boil this until it is reduced by about three-quarters. After that, add the stock and the pistachios and reduce until thick. Now let it cool.

Once cooled, scrape the mixture out into a mixing bowl containing the minced meats. Season well and then add the egg and the parsley. Mix thoroughly, using your hands.

Lightly oil the terrine and line with clingfilm, leaving enough overlapping the sides to fold back over the top after filling the terrine. Line the terrine with the strips of streaky bacon, again leaving enough overhanging the sides to cover the top.

Pre-heat the oven to 190°C/375°F/Gas Mark 5.

You can now start to build the terrine. Place about a quarter of the minced mixture in the bottom and press it flat. Place 6 strips of duck on top, season and then repeat these layers twice; finish with a layer of minced mixture. Now fold the bacon over the mixture and place the bay leaves on top. Fold the clingfilm over and cover with a double thickness of foil. The lid of the terrine should fit snugly on top. Place the terrine in a roasting tin and pour in enough hot water to reach half way up the sides. Carefully put it in the oven and cook for 45–50 minutes. The terrine is ready when a skewer stuck into its centre for 10 seconds feels hot, then warm, then hot when run lightly along your finger. Leave to cool in the fridge for at least 24 hours.

To serve, turn the terrine out onto a board and unwrap the clingfilm. Cut it into slices about 8 mm (3/8 in) thick. Serve on a plate with a dollop of the chutney. For a quick lunch, add salad or dressed leaves.

FOR THE CHUTNEY:

50 g (2 oz) butter
1 large onion, finely chopped
5 cm (2 in) piece of root ginger, crushed and then chopped
2 garlic cloves, crushed
1–2 tablespoons ground mixed spice, to taste
50 g (2 oz) tomato purée
1 tablespoon Worcestershire sauce
300 ml (10 fl oz) red wine vinegar
100 g (4 oz) brown sugar
5 large slightly underripe pears, peeled, cored and diced
100 g (4 oz) sultanas
100 g (4 oz) raisins
Maldon salt
Freshly ground white pepper

SERVES FIFTEEN

WARM SALAD OF CRISPY CHICKEN THIGHS

Chicken legs are not only cheaper than breasts but they can be made much tastier. The secret is in the slow cooking, which would leave a breast fillet dry and tasteless, When using legs you end up with crispy skin and succulent, well-flavoured flesh.

4 chicken thighs, weighing about 100 g (4 oz) each
2 tablespoons olive oil
1 garlic clove, lightly crushed
1 tablespoon lemon juice
150 g (5 oz) mixed salad leaves
1/2 red pepper, seeded and diced
50 g (2 oz) green beans, sliced into 1.25 cm (½ in) lengths and blanched
12 cherry plum tomatoes, halved or quartered
2 tablespoons Vinaigrette (see page 180)
50 g (2 oz) Olive Oil Croûtons (see page 184), optional
Maldon salt
Freshly ground white pepper

TO GARNISH:
Very fine shreds of carrot, optional
Long cut fresh chives, optional

SERVES FOUR

It's a good idea to buy boned chicken thighs but, if they are not available, you can bone them yourself. This isn't essential but it means they cook more quickly and are easier to slice once cooked. To bone them, run a sharp knife down the thigh bone, cutting into the meat to allow it to come away. Do this several times on each side until the bone comes free.

Heat a frying pan over a medium heat. Season the boned thighs well, add the oil to the pan, then place the thighs in it skin-side down. Toss in the garlic clove to flavour the oil. Now cook the chicken skin-side down until the skin is nice and crispy. This will take about 20–30 minutes. Turn over the thighs and discard the garlic, which will be well browned by now. Continue to cook the chicken for another 2–3 minutes. Add the lemon juice and shake the pan to make sure it is evenly distributed. Cook for another 3 minutes, then remove to a warm place to rest for 5 minutes.

To serve, place the salad leaves, pepper, beans and tomatoes in a bowl and season, then add the vinaigrette and toss well. Divide between 4 serving plates. Scatter over the croûtons, if using, then carve each thigh into 6 or 7 pieces and place them on top of the salad. Garnish with carrot shreds and chives.

WARM SALAD OF ROAST BEEF WITH SPINACH AND NEW POTATOES

This was devised one Sunday lunchtime when I realized I didn't have enough roast beef to use as a main course. My loyal fishmonger came to the rescue with some salmon and I used the beef for this starter. Native Scottish beef is far superior to Continental. Make sure it has been hung for at least two weeks, preferably three.

- 450 g (1 lb) trimmed sirloin of beef
- 2 tablespoons olive oil
- 15 g (½ oz) butter
- 450 g (1 lb) baby new potatoes
- 2–3 tablespoons mayonnaise
- 1 tablespoon horseradish sauce
- 100 g (4 oz) baby spinach leaves
- 1 tablespoon balsamic vinegar
- Maldon salt
- Freshly ground white pepper

SERVES FOUR

Pre-heat the oven to 230°C/450°F/Gas Mark 8.

Heat an ovenproof frying pan until very hot. Season the beef well, add the oil to the pan and pop in the beef. Brown well on all sides and add the butter. Now put the frying pan into the oven, making sure that the beef is fat-side down. Cook for 12–15 minutes, then remove and leave to stand in a warm place until the beef has relaxed and released some of its juices into the pan. This will take at least 30 minutes. But you could leave the beef to stand for up to 2 hours, provided it's not in too hot a place.

Meanwhile, cook the potatoes in boiling salted water until tender. Drain and leave to go cold. Thickly slice the potatoes and put them in a mixing bowl with the mayonnaise, horseradish sauce and some seasoning. Mix well to coat the potatoes, add the spinach leaves and mix well again. Divide the mixture between 4 serving plates.

Lift the beef on to a carving board. Use a very sharp carving knife to cut it into very thin slices. Fold these and pile them on top of the potato and spinach. Keep the juices that are released and scrape them back into the frying pan. Add the balsamic vinegar and mix well. Now spoon the hot oily juices over the beef and serve.

OVERLEAF:
Left: Warm Salad of Crispy Chicken Thighs (see opposite)
Right: Warm Salad of Roast Beef with Spinach and New Potatoes (see above)

Garlic Mushrooms on Toast

I used wild mushrooms in the television programme but this is a good opportunity to use big open-cup mushrooms. I'm assuming hungry people, so I'm allowing two per person. Real garlic lovers could add an extra clove or two, but don't sit next to me on the Tube!

8 large open-cup mushrooms
About 6 tablespoons olive oil
4 smoked back bacon rashers, rinded and diced
1 small onion, finely chopped
2 garlic cloves, crushed
50 g (2 oz) butter
3 tablespoons chopped fresh flatleaf parsley, plus sprigs of parsley to garnish
100 g (4 oz) fresh white breadcrumbs
Juice of 1/2 lemon
1 baguette
Maldon salt
Freshly ground white pepper

SERVES FOUR

Pre-heat the oven to 230°C/450°F/Gas Mark 8.

Remove the stalks from the mushrooms and chop them roughly. Now heat a frying pan until hot, add 1 tablespoon of the olive oil and put in the bacon . Stir-fry it until crisp, then add the mushroom stalks, onion, garlic and butter. Reduce the heat and cook for about 7 minutes, until softened. Add some seasoning, then the parsley and breadcrumbs and mix together well.

Oil a baking tray big enough to hold the mushrooms and put them on it rounded side down. Slather with about 2–3 tablespoons of olive oil, then season generously and add a good squeeze of lemon juice. Now divide the filling between the mushrooms. If they look a bit dry, don't be afraid to drizzle on more olive oil. Bake for 12–15 minutes and then start on the croûtons.

Cut eight 2 cm (3/4 in) slices diagonally off the baguette and lay them on a baking tray. Once again slather with olive oil. Be generous as the bread will absorb a lot. Season lightly and put them in the oven with the mushrooms. The bread will take about 6–7 minutes. Put the croûtons on 4 serving plates, put a mushroom on top of each one, then garnish with a sprig of parsley and a drizzle of olive oil.

Grilled polenta with a cep and tomato stew

The inspiration for this recipe came from a wonderful Aberdeenshire man named Renzo Serafini during the first series of *Wild Harvest*. I've changed it a bit since then but the original idea was Renzo's. Polenta is just Italian porridge and this dish brings the Italo-Scottish traditions together nicely. Polenta is often eaten runny but I much prefer it nice and thick. I let it set overnight, then cut it into slices and fry it in a cast iron griddle pan. Ceps grow all over Scotland and most of the UK from about mid-August to the end of October. If you can gather them yourself, do so. Good brown mushrooms or shiitake are an alternative.

1 litre (1¾ pints) water
225 g (8 oz) quick-cook polenta
50 g (2 oz) butter
20 g (¾ oz) fresh Parmesan cheese, grated
Maldon salt
Freshly ground white pepper
Olive oil
175 g (6 oz) rocket leaves, to serve

FOR THE STEW:
4 tablespoons olive oil
1 garlic clove, crushed
350 g (12 oz) fresh ceps, sliced
1 teaspoon dried basil
1 sprig of fresh thyme
450 ml (15 fl oz) tomato passata
30 g (1¼ oz) fresh Parmesan cheese, grated (optional)

SERVES SIX

For the polenta, bring the water to the boil in a saucepan, then pour in the polenta and stir until it thickens. Add the seasoning and cook until it gives off a nice, deep plop – about 5 minutes. Beat in the butter and Parmesan, check the seasoning and pour on to an oiled baking tray or large plate in a layer about 1 cm (½ in) thick. Leave for 3–4 hours, until cool and set.

Make the stew about 30 minutes before you want to serve it. Heat the oil in a saucepan and add the garlic and ceps. Stir-fry until well browned, no more than 5 minutes. Now add the basil and thyme and some seasoning. Pour in the passata, reduce the heat and simmer for 20 minutes, until nice and thick. Check the seasoning.

Now cut out a slice or two of the polenta per person and fry in a little olive oil for 2–3 minutes on a medium–high heat until each side is browned and a crust has formed. Serve with and a dollop of the sauce, and a little Parmesan scattered on top, if you like. Season the rocket leaves, toss in a tablespoon of oil and divide them between the portions.

Goat's Cheese Soufflés

Good goat's cheese from forward-thinking independent cheesemakers is becoming more accessible through specialist shops, delicatessens and even supermarkets. Its fine, deep flavour and interesting texture sets it apart from factory-produced counterparts. You need a ripe cheese for this. If you can't find goat's cheese, however, this soufflé is excellent made with Gruyère, Parmesan or a good sharp Cheddar.

- 40 g (1 1/2 oz) butter
- 2 tablespoons fresh white breadcrumbs
- 2 tablespoons finely grated fresh Parmesan cheese
- 25 g (1 oz) plain flour
- 450 ml (15 fl oz) milk
- Leaves from 2 small sprigs of fresh thyme, finely chopped
- 4 medium egg yolks
- 225 g (8 oz) ripe goat's cheese log e.g. Saint Maure, crumbled
- 6 medium egg whites
- 1 teaspoon lemon juice
- Maldon salt
- Freshly ground white pepper

SERVES SIX

Heavily grease six deep 7.5 cm (3 in) soufflé ramekins with 15 g (1/2 oz) of the butter. Mix the breadcrumbs with the Parmesan cheese and use to coat the inside of each ramekin – the butter will help the soufflés to rise and the breadcrumbs and Parmesan form a nice crust. Set them aside in the fridge.

Pre-heat the oven to 220°C/425°F/Gas Mark 7.

Melt the rest of the butter in a saucepan, add the flour and cook gently for 1 minute to form a roux. Meanwhile, warm the milk in another pan – it has to be warmed as cold milk can make the roux lumpy. Gradually whisk the warm milk into the roux and then add some seasoning and the chopped thyme. It is important now to cook out the flavour of the flour, so bring the mixture to the boil, stirring all the time, then lower the heat and leave to simmer very gently for 15 minutes – the surface should be barely moving. If it is cooking too fast, it will catch and burn.

Remove the sauce from the heat, pour into a large bowl and leave to cool for ten minutes. Then beat in the egg yolks and the crumbled goat's cheese. The base for the soufflés is now done. If you're not baking them immediately, dot the top with butter to prevent a skin forming.

Now whisk the egg whites to make the meringue for the soufflé. This is the engine that makes the soufflé rise. Put the egg whites into a large, clean bowl with half a teaspoon of salt and lemon juice and whisk until they form soft peaks. The tips of the peaks should flip over slightly, not stand upright. The soufflé mixture will need to be slightly slack so do not overbeat.

Spoon a quarter of the egg whites into the soufflé base and stir in. This loosens it up a little. Then gently fold in the remaining egg whites but don't overwork them. It doesn't matter if there are a few lumps or traces of white in the mixture.

Put the prepared ramekin dishes on a baking sheet and spoon in the mixture. Tap them gently to level the tops. Slide them into the lower part of the oven as the currents at the top tend to push the soufflé down (make sure the next rack up is not too close). Bake for 12–15 minutes until well risen and golden brown. You can check near the end of cooking but, whatever you do, don't open the oven door in the first few minutes. Serve straight from the oven. They may crack slightly on top but, don't worry, this is all part of the charm.

PARMA HAM, ROCKET AND PARMESAN ROLL

This is simple and easy but no less of a treat for that, since it contains some of my favourite ingredients. It makes a nice starter for a dinner party as you can make the rolls an hour in advance. Use mixed salad leaves if you can't get rocket. But it must be Parma ham and freshly grated reggiano Parmesan. Use the best olive oil you can.

- 4 tablespoons olive oil
- 1 tablespoon lemon juice or balsamic vinegar
- 8 slices of Parma ham
- 40 g (1 1/2 oz) rocket
- 25 g (1 oz) fresh Parmesan cheese, grated
- Maldon salt
- Freshly ground white pepper

SERVES FOUR

Mix the oil with the lemon juice or balsamic vinegar. Lay out the Parma ham on a board and spread the rocket on top. Scatter over the Parmesan, drizzle with a few drops of the oil mixture, then season and roll up. To serve, place 2 rolls on each serving plate and drizzle with more of the oil mixture.

PARMESAN BISCUITS WITH BABY LEEKS AND HOME-DRIED TOMATOES

These biscuits are so good that whenever I make them for the restaurant the boys in the kitchen have to hide them from the rest of the staff.

24 baby leeks, trimmed
12 Home-dried Tomatoes (see page 174)
25 g (1 oz) fresh Parmesan shavings
40 g (1 1/2 oz) fresh basil leaves
Olive oil
Balsamic Reduction (see page 178), to serve

FOR THE BISCUITS:
50 g (2 oz) butter
40 g (1 1/2 oz) plain flour
75 g (3 oz) fresh Parmesan cheese, grated
Cayenne pepper
Maldon salt

SERVES FOUR

First make the Parmesan biscuits. Rub the butter into the flour until you have a mixture that resembles breadcrumbs. Now add the Parmesan and a generous pinch each of cayenne and salt and work with your fingers until the mixture comes together into a dough. Then cover in clingfilm and leave in the fridge for an hour.

Pre-heat the oven to 200°C/400°F/Gas Mark 6.

Roll out the Parmesan dough until it is about 3 mm (1/8 in) thick and stamp out 4 rounds with a 9 cm (3 1/2 in) scone cutter. (Freeze the remaining dough or wrap it in clingfilm and keep refrigerated for 5 days.) Place on a well-oiled baking sheet (or one lined with baking parchment) and bake for about 8 minutes, until golden. Remove and transfer to a wire rack to cool (this stops them steaming and going soggy). Once cool, they'll keep for 24 hours in an airtight container.

Next poach the leeks. Bring a large pan of water to a rolling boil, then add 2 teaspoons of salt and put in the leeks. Have ready a bowl of iced water and a slotted spoon to fish out the leeks once they're tender, probably after about 2–3 minutes. Now refresh them in the iced water, then leave them to cool and drain.

To serve, place a biscuit on each serving plate and arrange 3 leeks and 3 dried tomatoes on top. Scatter with Parmesan shavings and more leeks. Place the basil leaves in a mixing bowl and season with salt and pepper. Add a splash of olive oil and toss well and arrange on top of the biscuits, leeks and tomato. Don't be tempted to do this in advance because the basil will wilt. Lastly, drizzle the balsamic reduction and more olive oil around.

Puff Pastry Filled with Chicken Livers, Mushrooms and Garlic Butter

A recent trip to Chablis threw up a starter of puff pastry with *foie gras* and baby ceps that was one of the best things I have ever tasted. This is my version with somewhat more available ingredients.

225 g (8 oz) puff pastry
1 beaten egg
2 tablespoons sunflower oil
350–450 g (12 oz–1 lb) chicken livers, trimmed
100 g (4 oz) brown or chestnut mushrooms, sliced
Lemon juice
Maldon salt
Freshly ground white pepper

FOR THE GARLIC BUTTER:

225 g (8 oz) softened unsalted butter
4 garlic cloves, crushed
15 g (½ oz) chopped fresh flatleaf parsley
Juice and finely grated zest of 1 lemon

SERVES FOUR

Make the garlic butter first. Place all the ingredients in a food processor and season well. Blitz for 30 seconds, then scrape down and blitz for another 30 seconds. Scrape on to a piece of clingfilm and roll up to form a sausage. Tie the ends and refrigerate to firm up.

Pre-heat the oven to 220°C/425°F/Gas Mark 7.

Roll the pastry 5 mm (¼ in) thick and stamp out four 7.5 cm (3 in) discs with a scone cutter. Brush with the egg and place on a baking sheet. Leave to relax in the fridge for 20 minutes, then bake for 10 minutes, until well risen and golden brown.

Heat a frying pan until very hot and add the oil. Season the livers and brown well on all sides. This takes 2–3 minutes. Remove from the pan and reserve on a warm plate. Add the mushrooms to the pan and stir-fry until browned. Add a little butter if necessary. Season and add a few drops of lemon juice. Remove from the heat.

Slice off the top layer of pastry and, using a sharp knife, cut out any undercooked pastry from the centre, leaving a 5 mm (¼ in) shell. Fill with the livers and mushrooms. Put 4 discs of garlic butter 1 cm (½ in) thick on top (freeze the remainder for another time). Replace the pastry lids. Give them a minute or two more in the oven. These are great served with a salad of herbs.

OVERLEAF:
Parmesan Biscuit with Baby Leeks and Home-dried Tomatoes (see opposite)

Seared Fennel and Chicken Salad with a Fennel and Tomato Dressing

We grow a whole pile of herbs outside Braeval in the summer – some more successfully than others. I've never had much luck with basil and chervil but rosemary, thyme and rocket thrive. However, the most prolific by far is fennel, and I'm always dreaming up new ways of using it. This salad can be served hot or cold. If you do serve the fennel and chicken cold, it's probably best to warm through the dressing to bring out the lovely anise flavour of the fennel. It also gives you a nice contrast in temperatures.

2 fennel bulbs, trimmed
65 ml (2½ fl oz) olive oil
Lemon juice
2 large boneless chicken breasts, skin on
Maldon salt
Freshly ground white pepper

FOR THE DRESSING:

1 teaspoon fennel seeds (optional)
120 ml (4 fl oz) olive oil
3 tablespoons chopped fennel fronds
2 plum Tomatoes Concassées (see page 181)
Juice of ½ lemon

SERVES FOUR

Poach the fennel in gently simmering salted water for about 30 minutes until tender. Remove with a slotted spoon and place in a bowl of iced water to cool. Drain carefully and cut each bulb lengthwise into 6 pieces. Try and keep a piece of the root at the bottom of each slice, as this stops the slices falling apart.

Heat a large frying pan until hot (a ribbed cast iron pan works well here), add half the olive oil and fry the fennel slices, in batches if necessary, until nicely browned. Transfer to a baking tray, season well with salt, pepper and lemon juice and keep warm.

Season the 2 chicken breasts. Wipe out the pan in which the fennel was fried and add the remaining olive oil. Fry the breasts, mainly skin-side down, over a medium heat until well coloured and cooked through. This should take 6–7 minutes. Now remove them from the heat and leave in the pan to relax for about 10 minutes.

Meanwhile, make the dressing. If using the fennel seeds, crush them with the edge of a heavy knife. Or you can roughly grind them with a pestle and mortar. Put the olive oil in a small pan with the fennel seeds and warm through for 3 minutes. Then add the fennel fronds, tomato concassées, lemon juice and some seasoning.

To serve, divide the fennel between 4 serving plates. Carve each chicken breast into 6 slices and arrange them on top of the fennel. If there are any nice cooking juices from the chicken, you can add these to the dressing, but check the seasoning as they might make it a bit salty. Then just spoon the dressing around the chicken and fennel.

If you prefer to serve this cold, simply put the fennel and chicken into a plastic tub and keep in the fridge until ready to serve. But do allow them to come to room temperature before serving.

GRATIN OF CHICKEN LIVERS AND PARMA HAM WITH PARSLEY, LEMON AND GARLIC

This simple recipe majors on big, robust flavours. All the work is done in advance and you can serve it simply in the cooking dishes. You could use any porcelain or ovenproof ceramic dish but I prefer the individual cast iron Le Creuset dishes. They're about 13 cm (5 in) in diameter and the perfect size for one serving.

- 120 ml (4 fl oz) olive oil
- Juice and finely grated zest of 1 lemon
- 2 garlic cloves, very finely diced
- 20 g (3/4 oz) flatleaf parsley, finely chopped, plus sprigs to garnish
- 350 g (12 oz) chicken livers, trimmed
- 4 slices of Parma ham, cut into strips 5 mm (1/4 in) wide
- Maldon salt
- Freshly ground white pepper

SERVES FOUR

Pre-heat the oven to 240°C/475°F/Gas Mark 9.

Lightly oil four 13 cm (5 in) gratin dishes and sprinkle with some seasoning. In a small bowl, make a dressing by mixing together the oil, lemon juice and zest, garlic and parsley.

Cut the chicken livers in half lengthwise and divide between the gratin dishes. They should almost cover the bottoms. Remember to season them. Now whisk the dressing and spoon it over the livers. Sit the gratin dishes on a baking sheet and put them at the top of the oven. They need 7 or 8 minutes. Once cooked, the livers should be still pink inside. You can give them another couple of minutes of you like but they'll be well done and grey. Remove from the oven, garnish with a sprig of parsley. Scatter the Parma ham and serve. Be careful as they'll be very hot.

Warm Salad of Peppered Venison with Cumberland Sauce

This works well with a nice piece of red deer. The meat needs to be from the saddle and trimmed of all fat and sinew. Don't get too carried away with the pepper; you only need a thin coating which should crisp up as you cook it. The first time I tried this I ended up with a quarter-inch layer of pepper – just a bit too much heat!

2 tablespoons black peppercorns, crushed
1 tablespoon white peppercorns, crushed
350 g (12 oz) piece of venison saddle
1 heaped teaspoon smooth Dijon mustard
1 tablespoon sunflower oil
25 g (1 oz) butter
275 g (10 oz) salad leaves
2 celery sticks, thinly sliced
2 tablespoons Vinaigrette (see page 180)
Maldon salt
Freshly ground white pepper

FOR THE SAUCE:
250 g (9 oz) redcurrant jelly
125 ml (4 fl oz) ruby port
Juice and finely grated zest of 1 lemon
Juice and finely grated zest of 1 orange
1/2 teaspoon ground cinnamon
1 teaspoon English mustard

SERVES SIX

The Cumberland sauce can be made well in advance. Put all the ingredients into a saucepan and bring to the boil. Skim away the froth and boil over a medium heat for about 30 minutes, until slightly reduced. Strain the sauce through a fine sieve and leave to cool. When cold, it should have the consistency of runny honey. It can be kept in the fridge for up to 8 weeks.

Mix together the crushed peppercorns. Smear the venison with the mustard and then roll it in the peppercorns – just enough to give it a nice thin coating. Season with salt. Heat a frying pan until hot. Add the sunflower oil and then the venison. Lob in the butter and reduce the heat to medium. Carefully fry the venison, turning from time to time, until it is well coloured and has a crisp shell. This should take 8–10 minutes. Now transfer the pan, vension and all, to a warm place and leave to relax for a minimum of 10 minutes (you can leave it for up to 40 minutes).

Put the salad leaves into a bowl with the sliced celery. Season, add the vinaigrette and toss well. Carve the venison into thin slices and lay these around the edge of each serving plate. Place a mound of salad in the centre and drizzle round the Cumberland sauce (I keep mine in a squeezy tomato ketchup bottle for this purpose, and it keeps for ages in the fridge). Spoon over any pan juices and serve.

AUBERGINE-STUFFED TOMATO WITH GOAT'S CHEESE AND A BABY SPINACH SALAD

The big flavours of firm, glossy aubergines and fat, ripe beef tomatoes should persuade you to give this Seventies dinner-party staple another try. The stuffed tomatoes can be made up in advance and finished in the oven before serving. Use the small, round goat's cheeses with a rind. There are now loads of shapes and sizes available in supermarkets.

The aubergine stuffing also works as a dip or to spread on toast or croûtons. Or try it with lamb.

- 2 aubergines, weighing about 350 g (12 oz) each
- 2 garlic cloves, crushed
- 5 tablespoons olive oil
- 4 large, ripe beef tomatoes
- 2 ripe goat's cheeses, weighing about 50 g (2 oz) each
- 100 g (4 oz) baby spinach leaves
- 1 teaspoon lemon juice
- Maldon salt
- Freshly ground white pepper

SERVES FOUR

Pre-heat the oven to 230°C/450°F/Gas Mark 8.

First make the stuffing. Cut the aubergines in half lengthwise and then score the cut surfaces in a criss-cross pattern. Cut as deep as you can without piercing the skin. Spread the crushed garlic over the cut sides and drizzle each with a tablespoon of the olive oil – the aubergines will soak it up at an alarming rate. Now sprinkle with salt and pepper. First make the stuffing.

Wrap each aubergine half in foil, place in a small roasting tin and bake for 20–25 minutes, until they are nice and squashy. Let them cool before unwrapping them, then scoop out the soft flesh. Put this in a mixing bowl and mash coarsely with a fork, seasoning well with salt and freshly ground white pepper as it can be a bit bland. If it seems at all dry, you can add some more olive oil.

Now stuff the tomatoes. Slice the tops off and, using a melon baller or a teaspoon, scoop out the flesh and seeds. Season the insides of the tomatoes well and spoon in the aubergine purée. Cut a thin slice off the top and bottom of each goat's cheese to remove the rind and cut each cheese in half horizontally to give 4 thick slices. Place one on top of each tomato and put them on an oiled baking tray. They're ready to cook now. If you like, this can all be done several hours in advance.

Reduce the oven temperature to 220°C/425°F/Gas Mark 7, put in the tray of tomatoes, and bake for 12–15 minutes. The tomatoes should be just soft and the cheese nicely golden. Give them a couple more minutes in the oven if necessary.

Put the spinach leaves in a bowl, season and add the remaining olive oil and the lemon juice. Toss to dress well. Divide the spinach between 4 plates, making a nice pile in the centre of each one. Using a spatula, lift a tomato on to the top of each pile and serve.

PART FOUR

FISH MAIN COURSES

Baked Dover Sole with Spring Onions and Ginger

The inspiration for this one came from my local Chinese restaurant. Oriental influences are now so widespread that there's something almost comforting and familiar about the flavours I've used here. Full of flavour yet deceptively simple. The sauce should enhance the fish without smothering it. Serve the fish in the foil parcels so your guests can savour the aromas as they open them up.

- 4 Dover soles, weighing about 225–275 g (8–10 oz) each, cleaned and gutted
- 150 ml (5 fl oz) sunflower oil
- Juice and finely grated zest of 1 lime
- 1 1/2 tablespoons Japanese light soy sauce
- 2 tablespoons dry sherry
- 4 spring onions, cut into 7.5 cm (3 in) pieces and then shredded lengthwise
- 2.5 cm (1 in) piece of root ginger, finely grated
- 2 garlic cloves, lightly crushed and then finely diced
- 1 small red chilli, seeded and very finely diced
- Maldon salt
- Freshly ground white pepper

SERVES FOUR

Pre-heat the oven to 230°C/450°F/Gas Mark 8.

Descale the soles by scraping them from the tail up towards the head with the back of a knife blade, then trim off the fins with scissors.

Take 4 large sheets of foil and lift the edges of each piece to form a large well in the centre. Mix the sunflower oil, lime juice, soy sauce and sherry together. Spoon a tablespoon of the mixture into each piece of foil and lay a sole on top, dark-side up. Season each one well with salt and pepper.

Now scatter over the lime zest, shredded spring onions, ginger, garlic and red chilli and then pour over the remaining liquid. Fold over the edges of the foil and scrunch them together well to seal. Place on 1 or 2 large baking trays and bake for 10–15 minutes, until the fish are cooked through.

Seared Sea Trout with Courgette Relish and Herb and Saffron Oil

Cooking fresh fish is a doddle. Definitely not something to be scared of. A good sea trout combines the best qualities of both salmon and trout but is better than either. Expect a glossy, firm fish with a delicate flavour, so keep things as simple and panic-free as possible. The relish is sweet and aromatic with a wonderful warm flavour.

If you haven't already, make the herb and saffron oils the day before.

The relish can be made in advance on the day you want to use it. Sweat the onions and garlic in the olive oil for 5 minutes, until softened. Add the sugar, tomato purée, balsamic vinegar, Worcestershire sauce and tomato concassées and simmer for 20 minutes until very thick, then remove from the heat. Fry the courgettes in small batches over a very high heat, using about a tablespoon of olive oil per batch, for about 1 minute until lightly browned. This is very important – if you cook too many of the courgettes at a time over too low a heat they will release their liquid, which will make the relish go runny. Season and then stir them into the onions. Leave for at least 2–3 hours.

To finish the dish, leave the relish over a low heat to warm through. Heat a frying pan over a high heat. Add a little sunflower oil, then add the trout fillets, skin-side down, and sear for about 2 minutes until crisp and golden. Turn over and cook the other side for about 1 minute, then season with a little salt and pepper.

To serve, place a pile of the relish in the centre of each plate. Drizzle the herb and saffron oils over the rest of the plate, then put the trout, skin-side up, on top of the relish.

4 tablespoons Herb Oil (see page 176)
4 tablespoons Saffron Oil (see page 177)
Sunflower oil
4 fillets of sea trout, skin on, weighing about 150 g (5 oz) each
Maldon salt
Freshly ground white pepper

FOR THE COURGETTE RELISH:
175 g (6 oz) onions, sliced
1 garlic clove, crushed
2 tablespoons olive oil, plus extra for frying the courgettes
25 g (1 oz) soft light brown sugar
1 teaspoon tomato purée
50 ml (2 fl oz) balsamic vinegar
1 tablespoon Worcestershire sauce
2 plum Tomatoes Concassées (see page 181)
450 g (1 lb) courgettes, cut into 1 cm (1/2 in) dice

SERVES FOUR

SEARED MONKFISH WITH CURRIED LENTILS

Curried lentils contain real layers of flavour and because they are cooked with plenty of liquid you won't need a separate sauce to go with them (see page 63). Get your fishmonger to cut the fillets from two large monkfish tails and trim away all the skin and fat so you're left with four perfect white fillets. The fish should be quite bright, slightly shiny and beautifully fresh. The curried lentils don't reheat too well (they absorb too much of the sauce) so prepare just before serving.

225 g (8 oz) Puy lentils
50 ml (2 fl oz) olive oil
25 g (1 oz) carrot, very finely diced
25 g (1 oz) celery, very finely diced
25 g (1 oz) leek, very finely diced
1 garlic clove, crushed and then finely diced
2 cm (3/4 in) piece of root ginger, crushed and then finely diced
1 teaspoon mild curry paste (or more if you like your curries)
300 ml (10 fl oz) Chicken Stock (see page 170) or Fish Stock (see page 169)
3 Tomatoes Concassée (see page 181)
3 tablespoons chopped fresh coriander or chervil
2 tablespoons sunflower oil
4 monkfish fillets, weighing about 100 g (4 oz) each
A squeeze of lemon juice
4 tablespoons crème fraîche
Maldon salt
Freshly ground white pepper

SERVES FOUR

First cook the Puy lentils in boiling water for 15–20 minutes or until tender. Drain them in a colander and spread on a tray to dry.

Warm the olive oil in a saucepan and sweat the carrot, celery, leek, garlic and ginger until soft. Add the curry paste and some seasoning and cook for 2–3 minutes. Stir in the lentils, then add the stock and bring to the boil. Add the tomatoes and 2 tablespoons of the chopped coriander or chervil. Check the seasoning. Simmer for 30 seconds, or until you have a loose sauce. Not too wet, not too dry. Then remove from the heat.

Meanwhile, put the sunflower oil in a very hot frying pan or ribbed cast iron pan and add the monkfish fillets. Fry them until well browned on both sides. If you leave them for 2–3 minutes before turning to cook the other side, this should prevent sticking.

Now remove the monkfish from the pan. It should be brown on the outside but still soft in the centre. Leave it to rest on a baking tray and season with salt, pepper and lemon juice.

Stir the crème fraîche into the lentils, which should be looking nice and rich by now. Divide the lentils between 4 warmed serving bowls, making sure the sauce is evenly distributed. Cut each piece of fish into 6–8 slices and place on top of the lentils. Garnish with the rest of the chopped coriander and serve.

Lasagne of Smoked Haddock and Peas

There is absolutely nothing wrong with comfort food. And this is as good as it comes. Perfect for those grim November days when it seems to get dark two hours after you get up. Try and avoid the radioactive orange smoked haddock. It seems to glow in the dark, so heaven knows what it tastes like. Fresh pasta is best for this but dried will do.

- 4 fresh or dried lasagne sheets
- 1 quantity Nage Butter Sauce (see page 172)
- 2 pieces of smoked haddock fillet, weighing about 175 g (6 oz) each, skinned
- 100 g (4 oz) good-quality frozen peas
- 2 tablespoons chopped fresh chives
- A few drops of lemon juice
- Maldon salt
- Freshly ground white pepper

SERVES TWO

It can be difficult to divide the portions when this is cooked in a single pan, so if possible cook each portion separately in a small pan.

Cook the pasta in a large pan of boiling salted water until *al dente* and then drain. Warm some nage butter sauce in each small pan until nearly boiling, then add the fish and simmer very gently until almost tender – about 3 or 4 minutes should do it. Turn the fish over carefully about halfway through as it will not be completely covered by the sauce. Now add the peas and the pasta and warm through for 2–3 minutes. Add most of the chives and a few drops of lemon juice, then check the seasoning and heat for a minute longer.

Now put the contents of each pan into a shallow heated serving bowl, rearranging the fish and pasta nicely and scattering over the remaining chives. Serve immediately, and forget that it's winter.

OVERLEAF:
Lasagne of Smoked Haddock and Peas
(see above)

Sea Bream with Zingy Couscous and Red Pepper Essence

Sea bream is admittedly an exotic fish but it's firm and fine flavoured. If you can't find any, you could substitute sea bass, red mullet or even salmon. As ever, get your fishmonger to prepare the fish fillets for you – it's his job. Couscous is just coated grains of semolina – a bit bland on its own but a perfect vehicle for other flavours. Here it has an Eastern feel but feel free to play about and substitute your own favourite flavours. The couscous actually benefits from being made the day before and reheated.

25 g (1 oz) butter
1 teaspoon coriander seeds
1–2 red chillies, finely diced (depending on how hot you like it; I use 2)
1–2 garlic cloves, crushed
4 spring onions, finely diced
450 ml (15 fl oz) Fish Stock (see page 169) or Nage (see page 168)
250 g (9 oz) couscous
2 tablespoons finely diced Japanese pickled ginger
Juice and finely grated zest of 1 lime
2 plum Tomatoes Concassées (see page 181)
2 tablespoons roughly chopped fresh coriander
2 tablespoons sunflower oil
4 sea bream fillets, weighing about 100 g (4 oz), skin on (but cut a few shallow slashes in the skin to stop them curling during cooking)

To make the essence, cut the peppers in half and discard the stalks and seeds. Cut a strip 2.5 cm (1 in) wide off each pepper and set aside. Chop the remainder. Heat the olive oil in a small pan, add the shallots and chopped peppers and cook over a gentle heat for about 10 minutes, until very soft but not browned. Then add the sprigs of tarragon and chervil and the vermouth and simmer until the vermouth is reduced by half. Add the stock and simmer for about 15 minutes or until the liquid has reduced by about half.

Now either give everything a quick blitz with a hand blender or pour it into a liquidiser and whizz for just 2–3 seconds, until coarsely broken down – you don't want it to be at all smooth. Tip the mixture into a conical strainer or fine sieve and press out the liquid with the back of a spoon into a small clean pan – you should be left with about 120 ml (4 fl oz). If there is more than this, simply boil rapidly until reduced to the required amount.

Dice the reserved pepper strips very finely and add to the pan with the chopped tarragon and chervil, seasoning and lemon juice to taste.

For the couscous, melt the butter in a large saucepan. Lightly crush the coriander seeds in a pestle and mortar and add to the pan with the chillies and garlic. Cook for 2–3 minutes, then add the spring onions and stock and bring to the boil. Season well. Now pour the couscous into the mix in a steady stream, stirring all the time with a wooden spoon. Don't worry if at this stage it seems a bit soupy and porridgy. Add the Japanese pickled ginger, lime zest, tomatoes and the chopped coriander and mix well. Remove from the heat, cover the pan and leave for 5 minutes, fluffing up with a fork halfway through, which will help the grains swell up nicely.

Heat a large frying pan until very hot, splash in the sunflower oil and add the bream fillets skin-side down. Cook for 4–5 minutes, until the skin is crisp but not burnt. Then turn and cook for 1 minute on the flesh side. Transfer the fillets to a baking tray and season with salt and pepper. Keep warm.

Now heat through the red pepper essence. Add the olive oil and lime juice to the couscous and mix well. Divide the couscous between 4 warmed plates or bowls and place the fish fillets on top. Spoon the sauce around the couscous and then drizzle a little more olive oil around the edge of the sauce so that it makes nice little pools.

50 ml (2 fl oz) olive oil
Maldon salt
Freshly ground white pepper

FOR THE RED PEPPER ESSENCE:

2 red peppers or 1 red and 1 yellow pepper
2 tablespoons olive oil, plus extra to serve
3 shallots, very finely chopped
1 sprig of fresh tarragon
1 large sprig of fresh chervil
3 tablespoons dry vermouth
300 ml (10 fl oz) Nage (see page 168)
1 teaspoon each chopped fresh tarragon and chervil
A few drops of lemon juice
Maldon salt
Freshly ground white pepper

SERVES FOUR

OVERLEAF:
Left: Sea Bream with Zingy Couscous and Red Pepper Essence (see above)
Right: Seared Monkfish with Curried Lentils (see page 56)

Baked hake with celeriac purée, red wine sauce and deep-fried Parma ham

Hake is similar to cod, though its superior flavour and texture warrant further attention. Deep-fried Parma ham is one of my favourite garnishes of the moment. I've used it with risottos, salads and game but it works best with a robust fish dish such as this one. You can deep-fry it up to 12 hours in advance. This recipe may seem elaborate but with a bit of planning the actual cooking and serving should be really quite straightforward. The purée can be made the day before and reheated at the last minute, and so can the sauce if you don't add the butter until just before serving. Baking is the easiest way to cook fish. Just get it in the baking dish ready to bang in the oven.

- Sunflower oil for deep-frying
- 4 slices of Parma ham
- 25 g (1 oz) butter
- 4 hake fillets, weighing about 175 g (6 oz) each, skinned
- 2 teaspoons lemon juice
- 6 tablespoons water or white wine
- 1 quantity of Celeriac Purée (see page 130)
- Maldon salt
- Freshly ground white pepper

Pour 2 cm (3/4 in) of sunflower oil into a medium-sized saucepan and heat to 180°C/350°F. Deep-fry the Parma ham slices, 2 at a time, for about 30 seconds, until nice and crisp. Drain them on kitchen paper and set aside.

Now make the red wine sauce. Bring the wine to the boil in a saucepan, add the treacle and boil until it is reduced by about three-quarters, to a thick and foamy syrup. Add the stock and boil until reduced to about 150 ml (5 fl oz), then whisk in the diced butter a few pieces at a time, swirling the pan as the butter melts. The sauce needs to be dark and glossy so don't use a hand blender to whisk in the butter as this would make it too foamy. Keep swirling until the butter has been incorporated, then season the sauce and keep warm. If it begins to look as if it might split, heat it up a bit and give the pan a good swirl.

Pre-heat the oven to 230°C/450°F/Gas Mark 8.

Heavily grease a baking dish with some of the butter and place the hake fillets in it. Sprinkle them with the lemon juice, dot generously with the rest of the butter and season. Add the water or wine to the baking dish and bake for 5–6 minutes. Meanwhile, warm through the sauce and the celeriac purée and have 4 warm plates ready.

When the fish is cooked, remove from the oven and baste with its juices. Put some celeriac purée in the centre of each plate, then put the hake on top. Spoon the sauce around the purée and place the Parma ham on each fish fillet. The soft fish, crispy ham, rich purée and glossy sauce complement each other beautifully.

FOR THE RED WINE SAUCE:

150 ml (5 fl oz) red wine
1 teaspoon black treacle
300 ml (10 fl oz) Nage (see page 168) or Fish Stock (see page 169)
40 g (1 1/2 oz) cold butter, diced

SERVES FOUR

OVERLEAF:
Left: Squid Tempura with Lemon Rice and Chilli Oil (see page 29)
Right: Baked Hake with Celeriac Purée, Red Wine Sauce and Deep-fried Parma Ham (see above)

Baked Trout Fillets with Glazed Leeks and Lemon Butter Sauce

Look for skinless, boneless Scottish trout fillets, preferably with the Scottish Quality Trout (SQT) symbol, and not just because of the flavour but also because they come thoroughly boned. The leeks are cooked to the stage where they are almost falling in on themselves. This intensifies and enriches the flavour. But they are not in any way heavy and work well with the delicate fish. The lemon butter sauce could be served with many other fish dishes. The trout should be cooked just right – that is, firm, moist and rich, and not overdone to a tasteless mush that refuses to stick to your fork.

65 g (2½ oz) butter
350 g (12 oz) large leeks, trimmed and cut into 2.5 cm (1 in) pieces
Juice and finely grated zest of 1 lemon
½ quantity of Nage Butter Sauce (see page 172)
4 skinless, boneless trout fillets, weighing about 150 g (5 oz) each
Maldon salt
Freshly ground white pepper

SERVES FOUR

Pre-heat the oven to 180°C/350°F/Gas Mark 4.

Place 40 g (1½ oz) of the butter in a small roasting tin, add the leeks and sprinkle over 1 teaspoon of the lemon juice and plenty of seasoning. Cook in the oven for 45 minutes, turning a couple of times, then remove and keep warm. Increase the oven temperature to 230°C/450°F/Gas Mark 8.

Make the nage butter sauce if you haven't already done so. Add the lemon zest and 1 teaspoon of lemon juice. Set aside and keep warm.

To bake the trout fillets, heavily grease a shallow ovenproof baking dish with some of the remaining butter. Season the trout and sprinkle with a little of the remaining lemon juice. Lay them skin-side down and then fold in half across the middle so that they form a loop. Place in the baking dish like this and dot with the rest of the butter. Add 2 tablespoons of water to the dish and bake for 6–7 minutes, until just cooked.

To serve, put the leeks on 4 warmed plates and carefully place the trout fillets on top. Pour any juices from the trout baking dish into the sauce and give it a good whizz with a hand blender or a whisk. Pour the sauce around the leeks and serve with mashed potatoes.

SEARED JOHN DORY WITH INSTANT NOODLES

Instant noodles are simple, easy and tasty, but this is not pot noodle. The secret is in the flavours that you add to them. It's impossible to resist a nice piece of translucent, straight-from-the-boat John Dory, but any firm-fleshed white fish would do as a substitute.

- 200 g (7 oz) egg thread noodles
- 3 tablespoons olive oil
- 1 red chilli, finely diced
- 1/2 red pepper, finely diced
- 3 spring onions, finely chopped
- 1 garlic clove, finely chopped
- 1 tablespoon Thai fish sauce (*nam pla*)
- 300 ml (10 fl oz) Nage (see page 168) or Fish Stock (see page 169)
- 1 tablespoon lime juice
- 1 tablespoon diced Japanese pickled ginger
- 2 tablespoons roughly chopped fresh coriander
- 2 tablespoons sunflower oil
- 8 John Dory fillets, weighing about 75 g (3 oz) each, skinned
- Maldon salt
- Freshly ground white pepper

SERVES FOUR

Cook the noodles first. Bring a large pan of water to the boil, add a generous teaspoon of salt and drop in the noodles. Remove the pan from the heat and stir with a fork. Leave to stand for 4 minutes, stir again, then drain in a colander.

Warm the olive oil in a large shallow pan, add the chilli, red pepper, spring onions and garlic and sweat for 1 minute. Add the noodles and toss well to coat with the spicy oil. Stir in the Thai fish sauce, nage or fish stock, lime juice and some seasoning. Toss well, then add the Japanese pickled ginger and chopped coriander. Keep warm.

Put the sunflower oil in a hot frying pan or ribbed cast iron pan, then add the fish fillets and cook for 2 minutes over a fierce heat until they start to curl. Turn the fish over and cook for 1 minute, then transfer to a baking sheet and season.

To serve, divide the noodles between 4 bowls, spoon round the juices and place 2 Dory fillets on top.

OVERLEAF:
Seared John Dory with Instant Noodles (see above)

Spaghetti with Crab, Chilli, Garlic, Parsley and Lemon

If you go to the trouble of cooking your own crab, make sure it's as big and firm as possible. Brown crabs are best, preferably ones that have big claws and feel heavy when you pick them up. The bigger they are, the easier it is to ferret out the delicious sweet flesh. I cook crabs in an unfashionable court-bouillon, or flavoured cooking liquid, as I think it improves the taste. I also cook them for a much shorter time than most people, who recommend 20 minutes or more. You could use frozen or pasteurised crab meat but for a dish as simple as this, fresh is best.

1 crab, weighing about 1.5 kg (3 lb) (see recipe)

FOR THE COURT-BOUILLON:

1 celery stick, roughly chopped
1 small onion, roughly chopped
1 carrot, roughly chopped
1 garlic clove, lightly crushed
1 bay leaf
1 small bunch of fresh parsley or herb stalks

FOR THE SPAGHETTI:

100 ml (3½ fl oz) olive oil
1 small red chilli, seeded and very finely chopped
1 garlic clove, finely chopped
Juice and shredded zest of 1 lemon
225 g (8 oz) spaghetti or linguine

The first thing is to cook the crab. Make sure it's alive when you buy it, then ask your fishmonger to kill it for you. If you cook it alive, the legs will fall off and overcook. Place the crab in a large pan with all the court-bouillon ingredients. Cover with cold water and bring to the boil over a high heat. Once boiling, simmer for 2 minutes and then turn off the heat. Leave the crab to cool in the cooking water. It will be just cooked, and the meat nice and moist.

Now comes the fiddly bit. Fish out the crab and discard the cooking water. Place the crab face down on a chopping board and give its back a good bash with the heel of your hand. This should open it up. Pull off the claws and give them a good bash with the back of a heavy knife or an old rolling pin. Pick out all the white meat from the claws, legs and body (the handle of a small teaspoon is useful for this). I usually stop there, as I'm not a great fan of the brown meat.

The rest of the dish is straightforward. You should have about 225 g (8 oz) of white crab meat. Place the olive oil, chilli, garlic and lemon zest in a large saucepan and warm through until just simmering. Then remove from the heat and leave to stand for 10 minutes (or you can let it cool completely and reheat it when you're ready to serve). Meanwhile, cook the spaghetti in a large pan of boiling salted water until *al dente* and then drain. Add the lemon juice to the olive oil and chilli mixture and season well, then add the pasta and warm through for 3–4 minutes. Add the crab meat and mix well, then the chopped parsley, mixing again. Heat until piping hot and divide between 4 warm serving bowls. I love it with a salad of herbs on top (see page 131) and a glass of chilled Sancerre on the side.

- 2 tablespoons chopped fresh parsley
- Maldon salt
- Freshly ground white pepper

SERVES TWO

SOLE AND COURGETTE GRATIN

I love this dish with mashed potato that has had a spoonful of pesto stirred in. Drizzle the mash with olive oil, scatter on some roughly torn basil leaves and you almost have a meal in itself. Make sure the fishmonger actually fillets the fish for you, as pre-filleted fish tends to hang around the shop and can resemble cardboard in taste and texture.

Pre-heat the oven to 240°C/475°F/Gas Mark 9.

Heavily grease a gratin dish with the butter and arrange the sole fillets in it, overlapping them slightly. Season well and sprinkle with the lemon juice. Lay the courgettes over the sole and season lightly. Scatter with the grated Parmesan and pour over the double cream.

Pop this into the hot oven and bake for 12 minutes, until golden and bubbling. Sprinkle with the chopped herbs and you're ready. It's great with mashed potatoes or some fresh pasta.

- 15 g (1/2 oz) butter
- 4 100–125 g (4–5 oz) lemon sole or grey sole fillets, skinned
- 1 teaspoon lemon juice
- 2 medium courgettes, very thinly sliced on the diagonal
- 25 g (1 oz) fresh Parmesan cheese, finely grated
- 150 ml (5 fl oz) double cream
- 2 tablespoons chopped fresh chives or chervil
- Maldon salt
- Freshly ground white pepper

SERVES FOUR

OVERLEAF:
Spaghetti with Crab, Chilli, Garlic, Parsley and Lemon (see opposite)

Shellfish Risotto with Ginger and Coriander

This method removes the mystique from making risotto and allows you to finish it at the last moment. This way you don't have to spend half an hour stirring away when you could be doing better things, such as drinking wine. Shellfish and ginger work well together and the coriander adds a fresh, zingy touch. Any shellfish combination will do but I prefer prawns and mussels. There's no reason, other than financial, why you shouldn't add scallops or lobster.

- 1.75 kg (4 lb) mussels, cleaned
- 200 ml (7 fl oz) white wine
- A little Fish Stock (see page 169), if necessary
- 85 ml (3 fl oz) olive oil, plus extra to serve
- 1 onion, finely chopped
- 2 cm (3/4 in) piece of root ginger, finely chopped
- 225 g (8 oz) Arborio rice
- 50 g (2 oz) butter
- 50 ml (2 fl oz) double cream, lightly whipped
- 25 g (1 oz) fresh Parmesan cheese, grated, plus extra to serve
- 1 teaspoon olive oil
- Meat of 3 scallops, sliced (optional)
- 100 g (4 oz) cooked, peeled langoustine tails
- 1 tablespoon roughly chopped fresh coriander, plus extra to serve

Heat a large pan until very hot and then put in the mussels and a quarter of the wine. Cover with a tight-fitting lid and cook until the mussels open, about 3–4 minutes. Discard any mussels that do not open. Shell the rest, leave them to cool and then store in the fridge until ready to finish the risotto. Drain off the mussel cooking liquid into a measuring jug and reserve. You need 1 litre (1 3/4 pints) so if it's a little short, make up the amount with fish stock.

You can prepare the risotto base up to a day in advance. Heat the olive oil in a large frying pan, add the onion and ginger and sweat for about 8 minutes, until soft. Then add the rice and stir well over a medium heat until it has absorbed the oil and become translucent. Stir in the remaining wine and 6 turns of the white pepper mill. Keep stirring for about 4 minutes until the wine has been absorbed. Now add 900 ml (1 1/2 pints) of the reserved mussel cooking liquid and bring up to simmering point. Simmer for 10 minutes, stirring from time to time. Then pour the contents of the pan into a large sieve set over a bowl to separate the rice from the cooking liquid. Quickly transfer the rice to a baking tray and rake flat. Leave it to cool, then put it into a plastic tub and refrigerate. Keep the cooking liquid.

To finish the risotto, put the rice, the reserved cooking liquid and the remaining mussel cooking liquid into a large saucepan. Bring slowly to a simmer, stirring from time to time. As soon as the risotto starts to thicken (after about 4 minutes), add the butter and beat in well with a wooden spoon. Once this is fully incorporated, add the cream and grated Parmesan and keep beating. Heat the olive oil in a small frying-pan and sear the scallops on one side only for 4–5 seconds. They should be slightly undercooked. Stir the langoustine tails, mussels, tomatoes, coriander and lemon juice into the risotto. Taste for seasoning, but the mussel stock will be fairly salty. Warm through for about 2 minutes. The consistency should be midway between soupy and stiff. If it is too thick, add a bit more stock.

Now divide the risotto between warm serving bowls and sprinkle with Parmesan shavings, olive oil and chopped coriander. It will have been worth it.

2 tablespoons Tomatoes Concassées (see page 181)
1 teaspoon lemon juice
Maldon salt
Freshly ground white pepper
Shavings of fresh Parmesan cheese, to serve

SERVES FOUR

OVERLEAF:
Shellfish Risotto with Ginger and Coriander (see above)

Spinach, Ricotta and Anchovy Tart

I used 16–20 large anchovies for the photograph of this recipe: I covered the base of the flan with a layer and mixed the rest of them with the filling.

- 1 quantity of Savoury Flan Pastry (see page 185)
- 1 tablespoon olive oil
- 225 g (8 oz) spinach leaves, washed, large stalks removed
- 1 garlic clove, crushed
- Lemon juice
- 100 g (4 oz) ricotta cheese
- 3 medium eggs, beaten
- 300 ml (10 fl oz) cream
- 100 g (4 oz) large anchovies, left whole, or 50 g (2 oz) canned anchovy fillets, drained and finely sliced
- Maldon salt
- Freshly ground white pepper

SERVES EIGHT

Roll out the pastry, use to line a greased 25 cm (10 in) flan tin and bake blind as on page 185. Remove the flan from the oven and reduce the oven temperature to 190°C/375°F/Gas Mark 5.

For the filling, heat the olive oil in a large saucepan, add the spinach, garlic and a little seasoning and stir-fry until the spinach just wilts. Add a squeeze of lemon juice and then tip the spinach into a colander to drain and cool. Squeeze out the excess water, roughly chop and mix it with the ricotta cheese, eggs, cream and chopped anchovies if using. Otherwise if using whole anchovies put aside enough anchovies to cover the base, chop the remainder and add to the filling here. Check for seasoning.

Set the pastry case on a baking sheet and, if using large anchovies, arrange them at random over the base. Pour in the filling and bake for 30 minutes or until just set. Remove from the oven and leave to cool for 30 minutes. Cut into wedges and serve simply; it doesn't really need any accompaniment.

Smoked Haddock and Puy Lentil Tart

The earthy flavour of the lentils combines with the smoked fish to give a nice contrast of tastes and textures. For an even richer, more luxurious tart you could substitute finely diced smoked salmon for the haddock. This is nice served with a tomato salad.

1 quantity of Savoury Flan Pastry (see page 185)
50 g (2 oz) Puy lentils
300 ml (10 fl oz) double cream
750 g (1 1/2 lb) smoked haddock, skin and bones removed (finished weight 450 g (1 lb))
3 medium eggs, beaten
25 g (1 oz) fresh Parmesan cheese, grated
3 tablespoons chopped fresh coriander
Maldon salt
Freshly ground white pepper

SERVES EIGHT

Roll out the pastry, use to line a greased 25 cm (10 in) flan tin and bake blind (see page 185). Remove from the oven and reduce the oven temperature to 190°C/375°F/Gas Mark 5.

Cook the lentils in lightly salted boiling water for 20–25 minutes until soft. Drain and leave to cool. Bring the cream to the boil in a saucepan and then add the haddock. Cover and poach gently for 3 minutes, then remove from the heat and tip the contents of the pan into a large sieve set over a mixing bowl. Break up the fish with a fork and leave to cool. When cool, mix the eggs into the cream, then add the lentils, Parmesan, coriander and flaked fish. Check and adjust the seasoning but go easy on the salt. Dump the whole lot into the pastry case and bake for 25 minutes, until just set. Cut into wedges and serve warm.

OVERLEAF:
Clockwise from top: Celery and Parmesan Tart (see page 120); Smoked Haddock and Puy Lentil Tart (see above); Spinach, Ricotta and Anchovy Tart (see opposite)

LASAGNE OF SQUAT LOBSTER WITH HERBS AND TOMATO

Squat lobsters are too often overlooked in favour of larger shellfish, such as langoustines, which can command higher prices from restaurants. They are, however, a true bargain, and though they might be a bit fiddly their sweet, delicate flavour makes this my favourite of all the dishes we cooked on the second series of *Wild Harvest*.

1.5 kg (3 lb) squat lobsters
8 fresh or dried lasagne sheets
1.2 litres (2 pints) Nage (see page 168)
50 g (2 oz) very finely diced mixed vegetables, such as leek, carrot, celery and fennel
50 ml (2 fl oz) olive oil
2 tablespoons Tomatoes Concassées (see page 181)
2 tablespoons chopped mixed fresh herbs, such as chervil, chives and parsley
1 tablespoon lemon juice
Maldon salt
Freshly ground white pepper
Sprigs of fresh chervil, to garnish

SERVES FOUR

First cook the live squat lobsters. Have some well-salted water boiling hard in a pot large enough to take all the squatties. Plunge them in, cover and let the water come back to the boil. Count 2 minutes, then take them out of the pan and immediately put them into cold water. This stops the cooking process. Remember, the biggest sin you can commit with any kind of fish is to overcook it. Leave it as late as you can before you take them out of the shells, otherwise they will dry out, but don't leave them lying around for more than 24 hours.

Cook the pasta in boiling salted water until *al dente* and drain. Now pour the nage into a wide shallow pan and boil until reduced by half. Add the mixed vegetables and simmer for 3–4 minutes, then add the shelled squat lobster tails, olive oil, tomato concassées, chopped herbs and lasagne sheets. Season with salt and pepper, add the lemon juice and warm through for 30 seconds or so.

Divide between shallow serving bowls, giving everybody 2 sheets of pasta and an equal amount of squats and sauce. Take a bit of care here and you'll have quite an impressive assortment of colours and textures. Decorate with sprigs of chervil.

Baked smoked haddock with a home-dried tomato and herb crust and Hollandaise sauce

The fish and tomato topping is quite rich in this dish so the lighter the Hollandaise the better. This one has less butter and more egg than usual to make it frothy. Serve this dish with some new potatoes tossed in butter and chopped chives or mint.

- 4 thick pieces of smoked haddock fillet, weighing about 175 g (6 oz) each
- 8 Home-dried Tomatoes (see page 174)
- 15 g (½ oz) mixed fresh herbs, such as parsley, tarragon, chives, basil and chervil
- 175 g (6 oz) fresh breadcrumbs
- 25 g (1 oz) unsalted butter, melted
- Maldon salt
- Freshly ground white pepper

FOR THE HOLLANDAISE SAUCE:

- 2 large egg yolks
- 100 g (4 oz) unsalted butter, melted
- 1 tablespoon lemon juice
- Cayenne pepper

SERVES FOUR

Pre-heat the oven to 240°C/475°F/Gas Mark 9.

Place the fish fillets in a lightly buttered baking tin and put 2 home-dried tomatoes on top of each one. For the topping, whizz the herbs and breadcrumbs in a food processor for 2 minutes until you have nice herby crumbs, then slowly pour in the melted butter. This should bring the crumbs together without making them greasy. Season the mixture, then scoop it out. Spread the topping neatly over the fillets and add 2–3 tablespoons of water to the baking dish. Set aside.

To make the Hollandaise, bring a pan of water to a simmer and sit a stainless steel or glass bowl over the top so that it fits snugly. Make sure the base of the bowl isn't touching the water. Reduce the heat and add the egg yolks to the bowl with 2 tablespoons of hot water. Start whisking them immediately and continue until the yolks are pale, thick and fluffy. Draw your finger over the mixture. If it leaves a mark for a couple of seconds, it's the right thickness. Now slowly pour in the warm melted butter, whisking continuously. Add the lemon juice and season with salt and cayenne pepper. Leave over the water to keep it warm but take the pan off the heat.

The fish now goes into a hot oven for about 7 minutes. If, after this time, the fish seems cooked but the top isn't brown enough, give it a lick with a blow torch or fire it under a hot grill.

To serve, lift the fillets out of their cooking juices on to 4 warm serving plates and spoon a pool of Hollandaise sauce next to each one.

Seared Mackerel Fillets with Stir-Fried Vegetables and a Frothy Butter Sauce

This is my favourite way to enjoy mackerel. One of my favourite memories of filming *Wild Harvest* on Skye is fishing for mackerel with Jerry Cox. Great shoals of mackerel filled the bay and we were able to walk out of Jerry's front door, straight onto his boat and catch our supper.

50 g (2 oz) fine green beans, halved
50 g (2 oz) asparagus, cut into 5 cm (2 in) lengths
4 spring onions, cut into 5 cm (2 in) lengths
1 small courgette, cut into 5 cm (2 in) batons
250 g (9 oz) egg thread noodles
1–2 tablespoons sunflower oil
4 mackerel fillets, weighing about 150 g (5 oz) each
Juice of ½ lime
A few drops of Chilli Oil (see page 175)
1 teaspoon Thai fish sauce (*nam pla*)
½ quantity of Nage Butter Sauce (see page 172)
15 g (½ oz) fresh coriander leaves, finely chopped
50 ml (2 fl oz) double cream, lightly whipped
Maldon salt
Freshly ground white pepper

SERVES FOUR

Bring a pan of salted water to the boil. Add the green beans and bring back to the boil. Then add the asparagus and bring back to the boil. Add the spring onions and courgette, bring back to the boil and drain immediately. Refresh under cold running water to arrest the cooking and set the colour. Leave to drain on plenty of kitchen paper.

Bring a pan of salted water to the boil. Drop in the noodles, then remove the pan from the heat, cover and leave for 4 minutes. Drain and set aside. Add a teaspoon of the sunflower oil so the noodles don't stick together.

Heat a frying pan until really hot, add a splash of sunflower oil, then the mackerel fillets, skin-side down and fry for 4 minutes. Turn over and fry for 2 minutes. Transfer to a plate, pour over half the lime juice, season and keep warm.

Heat a little more sunflower oil in the pan, add the blanched vegetables and stir-fry for just 1 minute. Then add the chilli oil, Thai fish sauce, remaining lime juice and seasoning.

Now warm through the butter sauce and whisk with a little hand-held whisker until light and frothy. Add the coriander and whisk again, then whisk in the lightly whipped cream.

To serve, divide the noodles between 4 warmed bowls and spoon on the vegetables, then top with the fish, skin-side up. Refroth the sauce as much as possible and spoon around the edge of the bowls.

PART FIVE

POULTRY AND GAME MAIN COURSES

SADDLE OF HARE WITH WILD RICE, GAME SAUCE AND RED ONION MARMALADE

Each saddle of hare gives two loins and one loin is sufficient for one portion. Get your butcher to bone out the saddles and trim up the loins. He can then also hack up the bones for the stock while he's at it.

2 prepared saddles of hare
1 bay leaf
1 sprig of fresh thyme
2 shallots, roughly chopped
1 garlic clove, crushed
50 g (2 oz) button mushrooms, roughly chopped
2 tablespoons olive oil
6 juniper berries, crushed
150 ml (5 fl oz) ruby port
1 tablespoon sunflower oil
50 g (2 oz) butter
4 tablespoons Red Onion Marmalade (see page 179)
Olive oil
Maldon salt
Freshly ground white pepper
Deep-fried parsley, to garnish (see page 131)

FOR THE RICE:

225 g (8 oz) wild rice
900 ml (1 1/2 pints) water
1 small onion, quartered
1 carrot, sliced
1 bay leaf
1 sprig of fresh thyme

SERVES FOUR

Pre-heat the oven to 240°C/475°F/Gas Mark 9.

For the sauce, put the bones, bay leaf, thyme, shallots, garlic, mushrooms, olive oil and juniper berries in a small roasting tin. Roast for 35–45 minutes, stirring now and then until well browned. Add the port and scrape up all the bits from the bottom of the tin. Tip everything into a saucepan, add water to cover, bring to the boil and simmer for 1 hour. Pour into a conical strainer or a fine sieve set over another pan and press out all the liquid with the back of a ladle or wooden spoon. Boil vigorously, skimming off any scum, until reduced to 150 ml (5 fl oz).

Put the rice into a large pan with the water, onion, carrot, bay leaf and thyme. Season well, bring to the boil, cover and simmer for about 35 minutes, until tender. Some of the grains will burst but that's OK. Drain, remove the aromatics, cover and keep warm.

Season the loins. Heat a frying pan until very hot, add the sunflower oil, half the butter and the loins and fry for 2–3 minutes on each side until well browned but still pink in the centre. Leave to rest somewhere warm for 10 minutes.

To serve, gently warm the red onion marmalade in a small pan. Cut the loins into thin slices. Put the rice on 4 warmed plates and arrange the hare on top. Bring the sauce to the boil and whisk in the remaining butter. Check the seasoning and then pour the sauce around the rice and drizzle some olive oil into it. Spoon the marmalade on top and garnish with deep-fried parsley.

PAN-FRIED MALLARD WITH STIR-FRIED GREENS AND A WHISKY, SOY, HONEY AND LEMON SAUCE

The secret of success here is to get the sweet and sour balance in the sauce just right. Mallard is smaller than farmed duck, but leaner and much tastier. If you can't get mallard, use 4 small female duck breasts.

- 2 mallard, breasts removed and carcasses used to make stock (or use 600 ml (1 pint) Chicken Stock), page 170
- 2 tablespoons whisky
- 1 tablespoon good heather honey
- 1 tablespoon light soy sauce
- 2 tablespoons lemon juice
- Sunflower oil
- 6 spring onions, cut in strips
- 75 g (3 oz) fine green beans, halved and blanched
- 75 g (3 oz) asparagus, blanched
- 75 g (3 oz) sugar-snap peas, blanched
- 25 g (1 oz) butter, cubed
- Maldon salt
- Freshly ground white pepper

SERVES FOUR

Boil the stock vigorously until reduced to 120 ml (4 fl oz). Add the whisky, honey, soy sauce, lemon juice, and seasoning and set aside.

Season the breasts well. Heat a large frying pan until very hot, add a good splash of sunflower oil, then the breasts, skin-side down. Cook for 4–5 minutes until crisp and brown. Cook the other side for 2 minutes, leaving the centres pink. Remove and leave in a warm place for 10 minutes. Add a little oil if necessary, add the spring onions, beans, asparagus and peas and stir-fry over a high heat for 1–2 minutes. Season well. Bring the sauce back to the boil, lower the heat and whisk in the butter. Check for seasoning.

To serve, carve each breast diagonally into slices. Put the vegetables on warm serving plates, arrange the mallard on top, then pour the sauce around.

VARIATION

Roast the mallard bones for 30 minutes. Brown 25 g (1 oz) each of chopped shallots, mushrooms, carrot and celery in 2 tablespoons sunflower oil. Add 1 tablespoon tomato purée. Deglaze with 150 ml (5 fl oz) port. Add 300 ml (10 fl oz) beef stock, 450 ml (15 fl oz) chicken stock and bones. Simmer for 1 hour, strain and chill overnight. Lift off the fat and boil vigorously until reduced to 150 ml (5 fl oz). Add 1 tablespoon chives, 25 g (1 oz) finely chopped summer truffle and seasoning. Cook the mallard as above and serve on 225 g (8 oz) wilted spinach with mini fondant potatoes (page 124) and the sauce.

Cold roast chicken with feta cheese, rosemary, lemon and olive oil

Perfect for a picnic or an *al fresco* summer lunch, or as a winter starter to remind you of summer. This relies on good ingredients to make a simple dish great. Try to get a good free range chicken to roast and buy the best feta you can find. This is definitely an excuse to use your top-of-the-range olive oil. You can even make this up a day in advance as the flavours improve over time.

1.5 kg (3 lb) free range chicken
50 g (2 oz) butter
175 g (6 oz) feta cheese, crumbled into small pieces
Leaves from 1 sprig of fresh rosemary, very finely chopped
50 ml (2 fl oz) olive oil
Finely grated zest of 1 lemon
3 tablespoons lemon juice
Maldon salt
Freshly ground white pepper

SERVES THREE TO FOUR

PREVIOUS PAGES:
Left: Pan-fried Breast of Mallard with Stir-fried Greens and a Whisky, Soy, Honey and Lemon Sauce (see page 89)
Right: Saddle of Hare with Wild Rice, Game Sauce and Red Onion Marmalade (see page 88)

Try to roast the chicken a day ahead. Pre-heat the oven to 200°C/400°F/Gas Mark 6.

Push your fingers between the chicken breast and the skin to make 2 pockets. Stuff 15 g (1/2 oz) of the butter into each one and rub the remaining butter all over the outside of the skin. Season very well and put the bird on a wire rack over a roasting tin. Bang it in the oven and roast until well browned, about 1 hour, basting occasionally. Depending on your oven, you might need to cover the chicken loosely with a sheet of foil after about 40 minutes to stop it over-browning. Test with a skewer in the thickest part of the thigh: the juices should run clear. Leave until cold, then pull off the legs and use a knife to cut off the breasts. Ferret out the 2 oysters from the underside of the bird (these are little secret crackers of flesh). Using your fingers, flake the flesh of the breasts, thighs, drumsticks and oysters. Try to get nice long strands and don't forget the skin.

Pile all the flaked chicken into a large mixing bowl and add the diced feta. Whisk together the rosemary, olive oil, lemon zest and juice and some seasoning and add this to the bowl. Toss well, check the seasoning and keep cold until needed. Serve with a few dressed salad leaves and a drizzle of olive oil.

PHEASANT BREASTS WITH DRAMBUIE, MUSHROOMS AND CHERVIL

Cooking pheasant needn't be a grand affair, nor should it be reserved for Sunday lunch. You can pick up pheasant breasts very cheaply around Christmas time and this recipe couldn't be easier (it could even be made with chicken or guinea fowl). Pheasant can be a bit dry, so it works very well with a sweet, creamy sauce like this one. The chervil adds a subtle extra layer of flavour. Serve with stir-fried cabbage flavoured with garlic and some Mini Potato Fondants (see page 124).

- 4 pheasant breasts, weighing about 100 g (4 oz) each
- 2 tablespoons sunflower oil
- 50 g (2 oz) butter
- 175 g (6 oz) chestnut mushrooms, thickly sliced
- 85 ml (3 fl oz) Drambuie
- 450 ml (15 fl oz) pheasant stock or Chicken Stock (see page 170)
- 150 ml (5 fl oz) double cream
- 1 teaspoon lemon juice
- 3 tablespoons chopped fresh chervil leaves
- Maldon salt
- Freshly ground white pepper

SERVES FOUR

Remove the skin from the pheasant breasts and season them well on both sides. Heat a large frying pan. Add the sunflower oil and half the butter, then the pheasant breasts and cook them for 3–4 minutes on each side until nicely browned and cooked through. The breasts should still be moist in the centre; be careful not to let them dry out. Remove from the pan and keep warm.

Add the remaining butter and the mushrooms to the pan and cook for a couple of minutes, until lightly browned. Now add the Drambuie and the stock and cook over a high heat until the liquid has reduced by half. Stir in the cream and lemon juice and bring to the boil. Return the pheasant breasts to the pan, together with any juices, and stir in the chervil. Bring back to the boil and check the seasoning. Place one breast onto each plate and spoon the sauce over to serve.

Pot-Roast Chicken Paprika

This is one of the first things I ever cooked in my basement flat in Byres Road, Glasgow. Apart from spaghetti bolognese and chilli con carne, it was the first dish I had made with any degree of success. Nostalgia aside, it's a tasty staple that freezes very well. The better the paprika the better the dish, so either go to a reputable wholefood store or make friends with a Hungarian.

- 8 chicken thighs
- 2 tablespoons sunflower oil
- 25 g (1 oz) butter
- 1 onion, sliced
- 1 garlic clove, crushed
- 1 large red pepper, seeded and cut into 5 mm (1/4 in) dice
- 1 teaspoon paprika
- 1 teaspoon redcurrant jelly
- 200 g (7 oz) can of chopped tomatoes
- 1 teaspoon tomato purée
- 1/2 teaspoon chopped fresh thyme leaves
- 600 ml (1 pint) Chicken Stock (see page 170)
- 350 g (12 oz) potatoes, peeled and cut into 1 cm (1/2 in) dice
- 2 tablespoons Shallot and Tarragon Butter (see page 178)
- 4 tablespoons crème fraîche
- 2 tablespoons chopped fresh chives
- Maldon salt
- Freshly ground white pepper

SERVES FOUR

Pre-heat the oven to 180°C/350°F/Gas Mark 4.

Bone the chicken thighs (see page 36) and cut each one into 4 even-sized pieces. Heat a large frying pan until very hot. Add the oil and enough pieces of chicken just to cover the base of the pan – don't crowd it or the temperature will drop and the chicken will end up stewing. Fry over a high heat, turning now and then, until golden brown. Season well and spoon into a casserole dish. Fry the remaining chicken in the same way.

Add the butter to the frying pan, together with the onion, garlic, red pepper and paprika, and fry for about 5 minutes. Add the redcurrant jelly, chopped tomatoes and tomato purée and cook for 2 minutes. Now stir in the chopped thyme and the stock. Season well and simmer for 5 minutes. Pour the mixture over the chicken pieces and stir in the diced potatoes. Cover with a tight-fitting lid and bake for 35 minutes, until the chicken and potatoes are tender.

Stir the shallot and tarragon butter into the pot roast until melted and then serve straight away in warmed bowls, topped with the crème fraîche and chives. It's fine on it's own but also very good with pasta or new potatoes.

Stir-fried Chicken with Mangetout, Chilli and Lime

Don't be put off by the fact that this is a simple stir-fry. It's really a question of using the right ingredients in the right way, and you end up with a light, colourful dish with great texture. The method is quite versatile and would work well with other stir-fry variations.

- 150 ml (5 fl oz) Nage (see page 168) or Chicken Stock (see page 170)
- 1 tablespoon runny honey
- 1 tablespoon Japanese soy sauce
- Juice and finely grated zest of 1 lime
- 1 red chilli, seeded and very finely diced
- 1 garlic clove, crushed and then finely chopped
- 1 teaspoon cornflour
- 3 tablespoons sunflower oil
- 4 chicken breasts, skinned, boned and thinly sliced
- 100 g (4 oz) mangetout
- 2 tablespoons roughly chopped fresh coriander
- 1 tablespoon Japanese pickled ginger, finely chopped
- Maldon salt
- Freshly ground white pepper

SERVES FOUR

Mix together the stock, honey, soy sauce, lime juice and zest, chilli and garlic. Mix the cornflour to a smooth paste with a little cold water, then stir it into the sauce mixture with a little seasoning and set aside.

Heat the sunflower oil in a large frying pan or wok and stir-fry the chicken in 2 or 3 batches until well coloured and cooked through. Lift it out with a slotted spoon and set aside.

Add the mangetout to the pan and stir-fry for 30 seconds, then lift out and set aside with the chicken. Stir the sauce to make sure that the cornflour is well mixed in. Pour it into the pan and bring to the boil, stirring all the time, then lower the heat and simmer for 2–3 minutes, until thickened.

Stir the chicken and mangetout back into the sauce with the chopped coriander and pickled ginger. Simmer for 1–2 minutes, until the chicken is heated through. Check the seasoning and then serve, accompanied by steamed rice or noodles and a crisp salad.

RISOTTO OF CHICKEN LIVERS, BACON AND CHIVES

Chicken livers are about 50p per pound, yet people overlook them in favour of *foie gras*, which is about 40 times the price. Is it 40 times as good? I doubt it. This dish is cheap and very tasty.

- 100 ml (3½ fl oz) olive oil
- 1 medium onion, finely diced
- 1–2 garlic cloves, crushed and diced
- 225 g (8 oz) Arborio rice
- 150 ml (5 fl oz) white wine
- 900 ml (1 ½ pints) Chicken Stock (see page 170)
- 4 smoked back or streaky bacon rashers, rinded
- 50 g (2 oz) butter
- 450 g (1 lb) chicken livers, trimmed
- 25 g (1 oz) fresh Parmesan cheese, grated
- Finely chopped fresh chives, plus a few long-cut chives to garnish
- Maldon salt
- Freshly ground white pepper

SERVES FOUR

The risotto base can be made up in advance. Heat all but a tablespoon of the olive oil in a large frying pan, add the onion and garlic and sweat over a medium heat for 6–8 minutes, until soft. Then add the rice and stir well until it has absorbed the oil and become translucent. Add the wine and 6 turns of the pepper mill and cook over a medium heat for about 4 minutes, until the wine has been absorbed. Pour in 750 ml (1¼ pints) of the chicken stock and bring to the boil, stirring from time to time. Reduce the heat to a simmer and cook for 10 minutes, stirring occasionally. Now pour the contents of the pan into a large sieve set over a bowl. This separates the rice from the cooking liquid. Quickly transfer the rice to a baking tray and rake flat. Leave the rice to cool, then put it into a plastic tub and refrigerate. Reserve the cooking liquid.

Heat a frying pan until hot, add the reserved olive oil and fry the bacon over a medium heat until crisp. Remove and drain on kitchen paper. Add 20 g (¾ oz) of the butter to the pan and, when it is foaming, season the livers and add to the pan. Fry for about a minute on each side until well browned all over but still pink in the middle, then transfer to a dish and keep warm.

Combine the rice, the remaining stock and the reserved cooking liquid in a pan. Bring them to a simmer and warm through for about 4 minutes. Mix in the remaining butter, then finely chop the bacon and add to the risotto. Beat in the Parmesan and chives. Check the seasoning, but go easy on the salt as the bacon and Parmesan are already quite salty. Now divide between serving bowls and place the chicken livers on top. Garnish with a few long-cut chives.

Poached Guinea Fowl Breasts with Leeks and Prunes

This is an upwardly mobile cock-a-leekie soup, with a few extra flavours and textures for good measure. However, it's not show-off cuisine, just very satisfying cooking and yet low in fat. It goes to show that low-fat food can also be tasty. Poaching the guinea fowl in the stock reinforces the flavour. I like to serve it with mashed or dauphinoise potatoes to soak up all the juices.

- 900 ml (1 1/2 pints) Chicken Stock (see page 170)
- 4 guinea fowl breasts, weighing about 150 g (5 oz) each, skinned
- 12 baby leeks, each cut into 3
- 8 large Agen or Californian prunes, halved and stoned
- 2 tablespoons chopped fresh tarragon
- 4 tablespoons cooked pearl barley (optional)
- Maldon salt
- Freshly ground white pepper

SERVES FOUR

Put the chicken stock in a large, shallow pan with a lid and bring to the boil. Season the skinned guinea fowl breasts well, then add them to the boiling stock together with the leeks. Reduce the heat, cover and simmer gently for 5 minutes. Stir in the prunes and tarragon, and the cooked barley if using. Bring back to a simmer and cook for 3 minutes. Check for seasoning. Now simply divide the stock, guinea fowl, leeks and prunes between 4 large shallow bowls and serve.

OVERLEAF:
Left: Risotto of Chicken Livers, Bacon and Chives (see opposite)
Right: Grilled Polenta with a Cep and Tomato Stew (see page 41)

Roast chicken livers and bacon with Parmesan and chive mash and red onion gravy

This is liver, bacon and onions with knobs on. Each ingredient has been given a little extra to make this an addictively tasty dish that also makes a good starter. Chicken livers are one of the last remaining cheap luxury items, and I can't seem to get enough them. The mash, too, is rich and creamy and marries well with the sweet, textured gravy.

2 tablespoons olive oil
4 rindless streaky bacon rashers, halved
350 g (12 oz) chicken livers, trimmed
Maldon salt
Freshly ground white pepper

FOR THE GRAVY:
4 teaspoons red wine vinegar
1 tablespoon redcurrant jelly
400 ml (14 fl oz) Chicken Stock (see page 170)
2 tablespoons Red Onion Marmalade (see page 179)

FOR THE MASH:
450 g (1 lb) floury potatoes, such as King Edward, peeled and cut into chunks
40 g (1 1/2 oz) butter
25 g (1 oz) fresh Parmesan cheese, finely grated
1 tablespoon chopped fresh chives, plus a few long-cut chives to garnish

SERVES FOUR

First make the gravy. Put the vinegar and redcurrant jelly into a small pan and leave over a gentle heat until the jelly has melted. Raise the heat and boil until thick. Add the chicken stock and boil until reduced by half. Stir in the red onion marmalade and boil until it has reduced to 150 ml (5 fl oz) and thickened. Season well and set aside.

For the mash, cook the potatoes in boiling salted water until tender. Drain well, return to the pan and mash with the butter until smooth. Stir in the Parmesan, chives and some seasoning, then set aside and keep warm. It will keep for up to an hour.

Heat a large frying pan until very hot, then add the olive oil and the halved bacon rashers. Fry the bacon for 1–2 minutes on each side, until crisp and golden. Set aside and keep warm. Season the chicken livers well with salt and pepper, add to the pan (don't crowd the pan; cook the livers in batches if your frying pan is not very large) and cook for just 1 minute on each side – you want the outsides to become lightly browned but the insides to remain pink and juicy.

To serve, pile the mash into the centre of 4 warmed plates. Spoon the chicken livers on top of the mash and then top off with 2 pieces of crisp bacon. Spoon the red onion gravy around the outside and garnish with some long-cut chives.

PART SIX

MEAT MAIN COURSES

Casseroled lamb with red wine and rosemary

This harks back to the time when a stew was a stew and custard was lumpy. Deeply unfashionable but none the worse for that. If you have a slow cooker lying at the back of your kitchen cupboard it's a good idea to use it for this. The meat will be cooked at a slow, even temperature, leaving it tender enough to cut with a spoon. Have a good red Rioja on standby to complement the rich juices of the sauce.

- 450 g (1 lb) boned leg of lamb, cut into 2 cm (3/4 in) cubes
- 2 tablespoons plain flour seasoned with salt and pepper
- 1 tablespoon olive oil
- 25 g (1 oz) butter
- 1 tablespoon tomato purée
- 300 ml (10 fl oz) red wine
- 300 ml (10 fl oz) Beef Stock (see page 171)
- Leaves from 1 sprig of fresh rosemary, finely chopped
- 1 garlic clove, crushed
- 1 carrot, cut into 1 cm (1/2 in) dice
- 1 onion, cut into 1 cm (1/2 in) dice
- 2 celery sticks, cut into 1 cm (1/2 in) dice
- Maldon salt
- Freshly ground white pepper

SERVES FOUR

Pre-heat the oven to 180°C/350°F/Gas Mark 4.

Put the cubes of lamb in a plastic bag with the seasoned flour and give the bag a good shake so that the meat becomes well coated with the flour. Heat a large frying pan until very hot. Add the oil and the butter, then the lamb and fry over a high heat, stirring now and then, until all the pieces of lamb are well browned. Don't crowd the pan; cook in batches if necessary. Transfer to a casserole dish and set aside.

Add the tomato purée and red wine to the pan and bring to the boil, scraping up all the little bits that have stuck to the bottom. Pour this into the casserole dish and add the stock, rosemary, garlic and diced vegetables. Add a little seasoning, cover with a tight-fitting lid and bake for 1 1/2 hours or until tender. Remove from the oven and check the seasoning. Serve with pasta or crushed potatoes (see page 124).

Braised Shoulder of Beef with Ale, Onions and Bacon

I can think of nothing better to raise my spirits than a generous portion of this casserole. Braising doesn't suit every cut of meat but it works well with cheaper ones, such as shoulder of beef. The meat is browned in a separate pan before adding it to the casserole as it needs a good colour to seal in the flavour. Good smoked streaky bacon will add another layer of flavour. A winter warmer that barely needs thinking about, it's so easy.

- 40 g (1 1/2 oz) butter
- 2 medium onions, sliced
- 450 g (1 lb) shoulder steak, trimmed and cut into 2 cm (3/4 in) cubes
- 25 g (1 oz) plain flour seasoned with salt and pepper
- 1 tablespoon sunflower oil
- 100 g (4 oz) streaky bacon in one piece, cut into lardons (short strips) 5 mm (1/4 in) thick
- 400 ml (14 fl oz) bottle of Scottish ale
- 1 tablespoon chopped fresh parsley
- Maldon salt
- Freshly ground white pepper

SERVES FOUR

Pre-heat the oven to 180°C/350°F/Gas Mark 4.

Melt 25 g (1 oz) of the butter in a flameproof casserole dish. Add the onions and fry over a high heat for about 5 minutes, until nicely golden, then remove from the heat. Meanwhile, put the beef into a polythene bag with the seasoned flour and toss together so that it becomes well coated.

Heat a large frying pan until very hot. Add the sunflower oil, then the bacon and stir-fry for a few minutes until richly golden. Remove with a slotted spoon and add to the onions in the casserole. Add the beef and the remaining butter to the frying pan and brown the meat well on all sides. Transfer to the casserole. Now add the beer to the frying-pan, bring to the boil and scrape up all the browned bits from the bottom of the pan – these will help to flavour the sauce. Pour this into the casserole, add plenty of seasoning, especially pepper, and mix together well.

Cover the casserole with a tight-fitting lid and bake for 1–1 1/2 hours. Now all you have to do is stir in the chopped parsley, check the seasoning and serve with lots of mashed potatoes and some green vegetables.

Roast loin of lamb with spicy couscous and an apricot and mint sauce

The wonderful flavours of spices in North African cookery hold a strange fascination for me. I love the combination of spice and sweetness without the heat of chillies. Cinnamon should be the dominant flavour in this dish but look out for the clean taste of mint, too. The warm, spicy couscous is another current favourite of mine.

450 g (1 lb) loin of lamb, skinless and boneless
4 tablespoons olive oil
Leaves from 1 large sprig of fresh rosemary
2 garlic cloves, crushed
Maldon salt
Freshly ground white pepper
flatleaf parsley sprigs, to garnish
Balsamic Reduction, to serve (see page 178)

FOR THE APRICOT AND MINT SAUCE:

25 g (1 oz) butter
75 g (3 oz) shallots, very thinly sliced
1 garlic clove, crushed
1 teaspoon ground cinnamon
1 teaspoon ground coriander
1/2 teaspoon ground turmeric
1/2 teaspoon ground cumin
1 teaspoon light soft brown sugar
50 g (2 oz) no-need-to-soak dried apricots, finely diced

Place the loin of lamb in a shallow dish. Mix together the olive oil, rosemary leaves and garlic. Pour this over the lamb, cover and chill to marinate for up to 12 hours.

Now make the sauce. Melt the butter in a small pan, add the shallots and garlic and fry gently for about 4 minutes, until softened. Add the spices and sugar and cook for 2 minutes, then stir in the dried apricots and stock, cover and simmer gently for 15–20 minutes. Add the mint and then either give everything a quick blitz with a hand blender or liquidise until smooth. If the sauce looks too thick, thin down to a pouring consistency with a little more stock. Check the seasoning and keep warm.

For the spicy couscous, melt the butter in a large pan. Add the spices and fry gently for 1 minute. Stir in the sugar and stock and bring the mixture to the boil. Add the raisins, pine kernels and then the couscous, stirring constantly. Remove the pan from the heat, cover with a tight-fitting lid and set aside for 5 minutes, giving everything a gentle stir with a fork halfway through. Lightly stir in the olive oil, lemon juice and chopped coriander. Cover and keep warm.

Heat a large frying pan until hot. Lift the lamb out of the marinade, season with salt and pepper on both sides and then add to the pan and fry for 3–4 minutes on each side until well browned. Set aside somewhere warm and leave to relax for 10 minutes.

To serve, put a large scone cutter on a serving plate and spoon some couscous into it, packing it down well. Remove the scone cutter and repeat with the other 3 plates. Carve the lamb into thin slices and arrange, slightly overlapping, on top of the couscous. Pour a little of the apricot and mint sauce around the couscous and then trickle the balsamic reduction into it, to form an attractive pattern. Garnish with a sprig of flatleaf parsley.

300 ml (10 fl oz) Chicken Stock (see page 170)
1 tablespoon chopped fresh mint

FOR THE COUSCOUS:

25 g (1 oz) butter
1 teaspoon ground cinnamon
1 teaspoon ground coriander
1/2 teaspoon ground cumin
1 tablespoon light soft brown sugar
450 ml (15 fl oz) Chicken Stock (see page 170)
25 g (1 oz) raisins
15 g (1/2 oz) pine kernels, toasted
250 g (9 oz) couscous
4 tablespoons olive oil
1 tablespoon lemon juice
2 tablespoons chopped fresh coriander

SERVES FOUR

OVERLEAF:
Left: Roast Loin of Lamb with Spicy Couscous and an Apricot and Mint Sauce (see above)
Right: Roast Rump of Seam-boned Lamb with Crushed Potatoes and Olive Oil and Rosemary Sauce (see page 108)

Roast Rump of Seam-Boned Lamb with Crushed Potatoes and Olive Oil and Rosemary Sauce

Seam boning is mainly a Continental practice but, like many traditional butchery techniques, it should be more widely used. It splits the meat of a leg down into individual muscles (of which the rump is one), which gives you no gristle and an even texture.

Rosemary, garlic and tomato are lamb's traditional allies but it's a versatile meat and can successfully take on so many other flavours – anything and everything except lurid shop-bought mint sauce, really. It doesn't like heavy sauces, however, so I've given this one a refined, classic treatment. The olives and anchovies in the crushed potatoes work particularly well with the tender, pink meat.

- 1 tablespoon olive oil, plus extra to serve (optional)
- 450 g (1 lb) rump of lamb, plus 100 g (4 oz) of trimmings
- 1 small onion, finely sliced
- 1 garlic clove, crushed
- 1 tablespoon tomato purée
- 225 g (8 oz) can chopped tomatoes
- 300 ml (10 fl oz) red wine
- 300 ml (10 fl oz) Beef Stock (see page 171)
- 300 ml (10 fl oz) Chicken Stock (see page 170)
- 1 tablespoon sunflower oil
- 1 tablespoon softened butter
- 1 teaspoon finely chopped fresh rosemary or basil
- 6 plum Tomatoes Concassées (see page 181)

Try to make the sauce the day before, as this is complicated special-occasion cookery. It also makes it much easier to skim off the fat, which will have solidified on top.

Heat a large frying pan. Add the olive oil and the lamb trimmings and stir-fry for about 5 minutes, until well browned. Add the onion and garlic and cook for a further 5 minutes, until nicely softened. Slop in the tomato purée and the canned tomatoes, turn up the heat and boil off any liquid. Then add the red wine and boil for about 15–20 minutes, until thick. Add the beef and chicken stock, bring to the boil and leave to simmer rapidly for another 20 minutes to reduce and thicken a bit. It should be quite concentrated in flavour. Pour the sauce into a fine sieve set over a bowl and use the back of a wooden spoon to force it through. You should be left with about 300 ml (10 fl oz) sauce, so reduce further, if necessary. If making the sauce in advance, leave to cool and then chill. Lift off any solidified fat from the top

Pre-heat the oven to 220°C/425°F/Gas Mark 7.

Cook the potatoes in boiling salted water until

tender. Meanwhile, heat an ovenproof frying pan until very hot. Season the lamb well. Add the sunflower oil to the pan, then the lamb and the butter and cook over a high heat for 2–3 minutes on each side until well browned. The pan then goes straight into the hot oven for 7–12 minutes, depending on how rare you like your meat. Transfer to a warm place and leave to relax while you finish the potatoes and the sauce.

When the potatoes are tender, drain them, then return to the pan and crush coarsely with the back of a fork. Pour the buttery pan juices from the lamb into the potatoes and add the diced olives, anchovies and basil leaves. Mix them through well and adjust the seasoning if necessary.

Now you can reheat the sauce, adding the chopped rosemary or basil and the tomatoes concassées. Bring it back to the boil, check the seasoning and it's ready.

To serve, place a 7.5 cm (3 in) pastry cutter in the centre of one serving plate and fill with the potatoes. Lift off the ring and repeat with the other plates. Pour the sauce round. Then carve the lamb and place 3–4 slices on top of the potatoes. Now, if you like, pour a little olive oil around the edge of the sauce – it should form nice puddles. And that's it done!

Maldon salt
Freshly ground white pepper

FOR THE CRUSHED POTATOES:

450 g (1 lb) new potatoes, scrubbed
12 black olives, stoned and diced
1 tablespoon finely diced anchovy fillets
1 tablespoon roughly chopped fresh basil

SERVES FOUR

Beef olives

Although this dish reminds me of school dinners, it is great comfort food and is perfect served with mashed potatoes and gravy.

450 g (1 lb) piece of beef topside
4 slices of Parma ham
900 ml (1 1/2 pints) Beef Stock (see page 171)
50 g (2 oz) butter
2 tablespoons Red Onion Marmalade (see page 179)
Maldon salt
Freshly ground white pepper

FOR THE STUFFING:
25 g (1 oz) butter
5 shallots, finely chopped
2 garlic cloves, crushed
175 g (6 oz) button mushrooms, finely chopped
1/2 teaspoon chopped fresh oregano
1/2 tsp chopped fresh thyme
350 g (12 oz) good quality pork sausagemeat
85 ml (3 fl oz) Guinness
2 tablespoons fresh white breadcrumbs
1 egg yolk
Pinch of cayenne pepper

SERVES FOUR

To make the stuffing, melt the butter in a frying pan and fry the shallots until softened. Add the garlic and then the mushrooms and herbs, and cook for about 10 minutes until all the moisture has evaporated and the mixture has thickened. Remove from the heat and leave to cool a little. Mix together the sausagemeat, Guinness, breadcrumbs, egg yolk, cayenne, seasoning and mushroom mixture until well combined.

Cut the beef into 5 mm (1/4 in) thick slices and beat between pieces of clingfilm with a meat mallet until thin and even in size. Season and lay a piece of Parma ham on top. Place about 75 g (3 oz) of the stuffing at one end and roll up to enclose the filling. Secure with a cocktail stick. Repeat with the remaining beef and stuffing.

Heat a little oil and butter in a frying pan. Fry the beef parcels until coloured and then drain briefly on kitchen paper.

Bring the stock to the boil in a casserole dish, add the beef olives, then simmer for 1 hour. Lift the olives out of the pan onto a plate and keep warm. Pass the stock through a fine sieve into another pan and boil rapidly until reduced to about 150 ml (5 fl oz). Whisk in the remaining butter and 2 tablespoons of the red onion marmalade. Place the beef olives into the centre of 4 warmed plates. Spoon the sauce around the parcels and serve at once.

PEPPERED FILLET OF BEEF WITH STRAW SWEET POTATOES AND A SALAD OF HERBS

This is a simple dish but a real masterpiece. The pale pinky-orange colour of the sweet potatoes gives it a welcome twist. The steak is carefully fried and then coated in buttery, meaty juices. Just that. Heaven.

- 3 tablespoons black peppercorns
- 4 fillet steaks, weighing about 175 g (6 oz) each
- 4 teaspoons Dijon mustard
- 750 g (1 1/2 lb) pink sweet potatoes, cooked as for Straw Potatoes (page 125)
- 25 g (1 oz) Duck Fat (see page 173) or Clarified Butter (see page 181)
- 50 g (2 oz) unsalted butter
- 50 ml (2 fl oz) Armagnac or Cognac
- 4 tablespoons Beef Stock (see page 171)
- 3 tablespoons double cream
- 1 tablespoon olive oil
- Salad of Herbs (see page 131)
- Maldon salt
- Freshly ground white pepper

SERVES FOUR

Crush the peppercorns coarsely in a coffee grinder. Tip the pepper into a fine sieve and shake out all the powder. This is very important because the powder will make the steaks far too spicy. Now spread the peppercorns over a small plate. Smear both sides of the steaks with the Dijon mustard and coat them in the crushed peppercorns. Only now season with salt, because salting first would prevent the pepper sticking to the meat. Set aside.

Cook the sweet potatoes (see page 125).

Heat a large frying pan until hot. Add the duck fat or clarified butter and then the steaks and give them a couple of minutes on either side (a bit longer if you don't like your meat so rare). Do not move them around once they are in the pan or the peppercorn crust will fall off – the aim is to produce a good crusty coating on each surface. Now add the butter to the pan and allow it to colour to nut brown, basting the steaks with the buttery juices as you go. Transfer the steaks to a baking tray and leave in a warm place.

Add the Armagnac or cognac to the pan and boil over a high heat for 1 minute – the alcohol must be boiled off. Then add the beef stock, bring back to the boil and pour in the cream. Scrape and stir together any gooey bits from the bottom of the pan. When it boils, it's ready.

Dress the salad. Pour any juices from the steak back into the sauce and place a steak on each plate with a pile of salad and straw potatoes. Spoon the sauce over the steaks and serve.

Roast pork loin with stir-fried cabbage, butterbeans and bacon and a cider cream sauce

This is a bit of a high-wire act, balancing many flavours and textures. Make sure the skin of the pork is nice and crispy and, if you've got time, cook the butterbeans yourself, as they'll soak up the flavours of all the other ingredients. Otherwise, use canned butterbeans. Always use the best-quality dry cider you can find.

550 g (1 1/4 lb) loin of pork, boned and skin removed
2 tablespoons sunflower oil
300 ml (10 fl oz) dry cider
450 ml (15 fl oz) ham stock or Chicken Stock (see page 170)
200 ml (7 fl oz) double cream
2 tablespoons olive oil
4 rindless streaky bacon rashers
1/2 Savoy cabbage, core removed and thinly sliced
Maldon salt
Freshly ground white pepper

FOR THE BUTTERBEANS:

175 g (6 oz) dried butterbeans
1 bay leaf
1 sprig of fresh thyme
1 head of garlic, cut in half horizontally
1 carrot, sliced
1 celery stick, sliced
1/2 onion, peeled

SERVES FOUR

Soak the butterbeans overnight. Next day, cook the soaked butterbeans. Drain them and then rinse under cold running water. Tip into a pan and add the bay leaf, thyme, garlic, carrot, celery and onion and enough water to cover the butterbeans by 1 inch. Bring to the boil, skimming off any scum as it rises to the surface, and leave to simmer very slowly for about 40 minutes or until tender. Season with salt 10 minutes before the end. As soon as the beans are ready, drain them, lift out and discard the herbs and vegetables, and set the beans to one side.

Pre-heat the oven to 200°C/400°F/Gas Mark 6.

Trim the pork loin and slash the fat at 2.5 cm (1 in) intervals along its length, being careful not to cut right through to the meat underneath. Season the meat well on all sides.

Heat an ovenproof frying pan until very hot. Add the sunflower oil and then the pork, fat-side down, and sear for 3–4 minutes on each side, until well browned all over. Now put the frying pan in the oven and cook the pork for about 40 minutes. Check that it's cooked by seeing if the juices run clear when the meat is pierced with a skewer. Leave in a warm place to relax.

For the sauce, pour the cider into a pan and boil rapidly until reduced to 2 tablespoons. Add 300 ml (10 fl oz) of the stock and boil until reduced to 120 ml (4 fl oz). Pour in the cream and boil for a few minutes until thickened slightly. Keep warm over a low heat.

Heat the olive oil in a large frying pan, dice the bacon and fry until crisp and golden. Now add the shredded cabbage and stir-fry for a few minutes until it has softened but still retains a little bit of crunch. Stir in the butterbeans and the remaining stock and simmer for 3 minutes. Season well.

To serve, mound the cabbage in the centre of 4 warmed plates. Carve the pork into thin slices and arrange on top of the cabbage. Gradually add any juices from the pork to the sauce but be careful because they might make it too salty. Check the seasoning and then pour the sauce around the cabbage.

SPICED PORK FILLET WITH APPLES, RAISINS AND CALVADOS

Pork fillet is lean and good value but just a little bland. I've tried to perk it up here, in what is quite a substantial and spicy dish. You can save time by using ready-ground spices but beware – they don't last as long as many of us think. The golden rule is to buy little and often, and store them in an air- and light-tight container. We grind all our spices to order at the restaurant, using a coffee grinder. It's well worth the effort.

- 450 g (1 lb) pork fillet, trimmed
- 3 tablespoons sunflower oil
- 25 g (1 oz) butter
- 1 small onion, finely chopped
- 1 teaspoon ground cinnamon
- 1/2 teaspoon ground allspice
- 1/2 teaspoon ground ginger
- 1 tablespoon light soft brown sugar
- 50 ml (2 fl oz) Calvados
- 50 g (2 oz) raisins

Cut the pork fillet across into 2.5 cm (1 in) lengths. Lay a few pieces of the meat at a time between 2 sheets of clingfilm or dampened greaseproof paper and with a rolling pin carefully beat them out until they are about 5 mm (1/4 in) thick. Don't be too vigorous when you are doing this or your slices of pork will begin to fall apart.

Mix together all the ingredients for the spice coating and spread out on a large plate. You will have more than you need but it will keep in a sealed plastic bag until the next time you want to use it.

Heat a large frying pan until hot, then add the

2 Granny Smith apples, peeled, cored and cut into 1 cm (1/2 in) dice
150 ml (5 fl oz) Chicken Stock (see page 170)
150 ml (5 fl oz) double cream
Maldon salt
Freshly ground white pepper

FOR THE SPICE COATING:

2 tablespoons plain flour
1 tablespoon light soft brown sugar
2 teaspoons salt
2 teaspoons ground cinnamon
1 teaspoon English mustard powder
1 teaspoon ground cumin
1 teaspoon ground coriander
1 teaspoon crushed black peppercorns
1 teaspoon ground allspice
1 teaspoon freshly grated nutmeg

SERVES FOUR

sunflower oil. Coat a few slices of the pork in the spice mixture and fry for about 2 minutes on each side, until cooked through and lightly golden. Lift out on to a plate and keep warm while you cook the remaining pork in the same way.

Lower the heat under the frying pan and add the butter. When it has melted, add the onion, cinnamon, allspice, ginger and sugar and fry for about 5 minutes, until the onion has softened. Stir in the Calvados, raise the heat and bring to the boil, scraping up any bits that have stuck to the bottom of the pan. Add the raisins and diced apples and cook for 2–3 minutes. Then add the stock and boil until reduced by half. Add the cream, bring to the boil and cook for 1–2 minutes, until the sauce has thickened.

Check the seasoning of the sauce and then return the pieces of pork and any juices to the pan. Simmer until the pork has heated through. Serve with some boiled new potatoes and green vegetables.

PART SEVEN

VEGETARIAN MAIN COURSES

NORTH AFRICAN COUSCOUS WITH ROAST VEGETABLES

Just a handful of spices combines with a basic range of fresh ingredients to produce this kaleidoscopic and many-layered dish. The famed preserved lemons can be found in many delicatessens. To simplify the dish, you could omit the sauce and serve the couscous with just olive oil drizzled round it, as we did for the photo overleaf.

1 large aubergine, cut in 1 cm (1/2 in) thick lengthwise slices
25 g (1 oz) butter
1 teaspoon ground cumin
1 teaspoon ground cinnamon
1 teaspoon ground coriander
1 teaspoon ground allspice
1 1/2 teaspoons brown sugar
40 g (1 1/2 oz) pine kernels, toasted
75 g (3 oz) raisins
450 ml (15 fl oz) Nage (see page 168) or water
2 tablespoons chopped fresh coriander
250 g (9 oz) couscous
A few slices of preserved lemon, finely chopped (optional)
1 red onion, thickly sliced
1 red and 1 yellow pepper, cut into quarters
1 large courgette, sliced lengthwise
120 ml (4 fl oz) olive oil, plus extra for grilling the vegetables
2 shallots, finely diced
2 plum tomatoes, chopped
1 tablespoon lemon juice
Maldon salt
Freshly ground white pepper

SERVES FOUR

Put the aubergine slices in a colander, salt them well and leave for 30 minutes. Rinse well and then pat them dry.

Mix all the spices together. Melt the butter in a large saucepan that has a tight-fitting lid, add 3 teaspoons of the spices and the sugar and fry over a low heat for 1–2 minutes. Add the pine kernels, raisins, nage and half the chopped coriander and bring to the boil. Add the couscous, stir, then cover and remove from the heat. Leave for 5 minutes stirring half way through until light and crumbly. Season well with salt and pepper and add the preserved lemon if using. Keep warm until required.

Heat a ribbed grill pan until very hot. Use cocktail sticks to hold the layers of the onion slices together, if necessary. Grill the courgettes and aubergine a few at a time with plenty of olive oil and seasoning on both sides until well coloured and tender.

Meanwhile, heat the remaining spices in a small pan, then add the olive oil and shallots and cook over a low heat for 5 minutes until the shallots are soft. Add the chopped tomatoes, the remaining fresh coriander and the lemon juice and season well.

To serve, pile the couscous onto warmed plates with a tower of roast vegetables on top. Reheat the sauce if necessary and spoon it around the couscous.

Braised Root Vegetables with Pearl Barley and Tarragon

A lot of vegetarian dishes depend too heavily on Ital-Cal influences and they've become a bit clichéd. The inspiration for this recipe came from a little closer to home. I'll never replace bacon with Quorn in my frying pan, but I really don't miss the meat in this classic stew. It could also be served as an excellent accompaniment to game.

- 1 onion
- 2 carrots
- 2 celery sticks
- 2 leeks
- 2 parsnips
- 1/4 swede
- 2 large potatoes
- 25 g (1 oz) butter
- 3 tablespoons olive oil
- 40 g (1 1/2 oz) pearl barley
- 2 teaspoons tomato purée
- 1 tablespoon plain flour
- 600 ml (1 pint) Nage (see page 168)
- 2 tablespoons chopped fresh tarragon
- Maldon salt
- Freshly ground white pepper

SERVES FOUR

Cut all the vegetables into large chunks. Heat the butter and olive oil in a large saucepan. When the butter is foaming, add the vegetables and stir-fry over a high heat until well browned. Add the pearl barley and tomato purée and cook for 2–3 minutes. Stir in the flour, salt and pepper, then gradually stir in the stock. Cover and simmer gently for 25 minutes. When the cooking time is up, check that all the different types of vegetable are tender; if not, give it a few more minutes.

Stir in the chopped tarragon and simmer for 1 minute. Check the seasoning and serve.

OVERLEAF:
Left: North African Couscous with Roast Vegetables (see opposite)
Right: Braised Root Vegetables with Pearl Barley and Tarragon (see above)

Celery and Parmesan Tart

Of all these ideas for savoury tarts in this book (see also pages 80 and 81, and illustration on page 82), this is my favourite and probably the simplest and easiest. The secret is to cut the celery very, very finely, as it isn't precooked. It should still have a crunch to it, and the filling should be soft and cheesy. The celery could be chopped in a food processor but for best results, do it by hand. Peel it first to get rid of any tough fibres. If you'd like to serve this as a starter, it would do for 12 people.

- 1 quantity of Savoury Flan Pastry (see page 185)
- 350 g (12 oz) celery, finely diced
- 300 ml (10 fl oz) double cream
- 3 medium eggs, beaten
- 75 g (3 oz) fresh Parmesan cheese, grated
- 2 tablespoons finely chopped fresh chives
- Maldon salt
- Freshly ground white pepper

SERVES EIGHT

Roll out the pastry, use to line a 25 cm (10 in) flan tin and bake blind as on page 185. Remove from the oven and reduce the oven temperature to 190°C/375°F/Gas Mark 5.

Mix together all the remaining ingredients in a bowl and season well. Pour into the pastry case and bake for about 30 minutes, until just set. Don't over-cook it as it should still be slightly wobbly in the centre. Cut into wedges and serve warm.

Home-made noodles with pesto

This is the kind of dish that I eat at home, either for lunch, or as a night-time snack. Home-made pesto is a bit of a must with something as simple as this and this unusual one is a change from the familiar all-basil recipe. It can only be made in fairly large quantities but it does freeze surprisingly well. Freeze it in the compartments of an ice-cube tray and either keep it covered with clingfilm or put the cubes into a sealed tub once frozen. It should keep for up to 3 months. Home-made noodles are the very best for this but good-quality fresh or dried bought pasta makes it extra-quick and almost as good.

225 g (8 oz) fresh or dried fettuccine or linguine, preferably home-made (see page 182)
50 ml (2 fl oz) olive oil, optional
25 g (1 oz) fresh Parmesan cheese, grated
2–3 tablespoons roughly chopped fresh basil
Maldon salt
Freshly ground white pepper

FOR THE PESTO:
75 g (3 oz) mixed fresh basil, flatleaf parsley and rocket leaves
50 g (2 oz) fresh Parmesan cheese, grated
50 g (2 oz) pine kernels
3 garlic cloves, chopped
175 ml (6 fl oz) olive oil

SERVES TWO

Put all the ingredients for the pesto in a food processor and whizz for 30 seconds. Scrape around inside with a spatula and whizz again for a further 30 seconds. That's it.

Cook the pasta in a large pan of boiling salted water until *al dente* and then drain. Put it back into the dry cooking pan and add the oil, if using, and some salt and pepper. Toss well to coat the pasta. Now add 4 tablespoons of the pesto and toss again. Divide between 4 warm serving bowls and scatter with the grated Parmesan and roughly chopped basil. Stuff yourselves.

PENNE WITH TOMATO AND CHILLI SAUCE

Running a restaurant is an exhilarating, if exhausting, experience. It's nice to fall back on something this simple occasionally. However, the sauce doesn't have to be so straightforward. I've eaten it with lemon thyme noodles, fresh prawns and Parmesan. The ketchup is there because it adds a nice sweetness to the sauce. Add more of the explosive chillies if you want a real slap across the palate.

1 onion, finely chopped
1 red chilli, seeded and very finely diced
2 garlic cloves, crushed
4 tablespoons olive oil
400 g (14 oz) can of chopped tomatoes
175 ml (6 fl oz) tomato passata
1 tablespoon balsamic vinegar
1 tablespoon tomato ketchup
275 g (10 oz) penne
15 g (1/2 oz) fresh basil leaves, finely chopped, plus a few whole basil leaves to garnish
50 g (2 oz) fresh Parmesan cheese, finely grated
Maldon salt
Freshly ground white pepper

SERVES TWO TO THREE

Sweat the onion, chilli and garlic in the olive oil until soft and lightly coloured (I know it seems like a lot of oil, but don't worry). Then add the chopped tomatoes, tomato passata, balsamic vinegar and tomato ketchup. Bring to a simmer and leave to cook over a very low heat for about 45 minutes, until thick. Season well with salt and pepper.

Cook the penne in a large pan of boiling salted water until *al dente* and then drain. Add to the sauce with the chopped basil and toss well. To serve, divide the pasta between 4 warm serving bowls and scatter over the Parmesan and a few extra basil leaves.

PART EIGHT

POTATO DISHES AND GARNISHES

Crushed potatoes with olive oil, Parmesan and basil

This is a kind of textured mash so don't be tempted to make it too smooth. Use the finest new potatoes and the best olive oil you can find.

- 450 g (1 lb) new potatoes, scrubbed
- 85 ml (3 fl oz) olive oil
- 3 tablespoons roughly chopped fresh basil leaves
- 25 g (1 oz) fresh Parmesan cheese, shaved
- Maldon salt
- Freshly ground white pepper

SERVES FOUR

Cook the potatoes in simmering salted water until tender, then drain and place in a large mixing bowl. Add the oil and, with the back of a fork, gently crush each potato until it just splits. Season, then add the basil and Parmesan. Mix carefully until all the oil has been absorbed. Don't overwork it or you'll lose the texture. You can serve the potatoes in a pile or use a 7.5 cm (3 in) scone cutter to shape them into nice little cakes. The mixture can be made in advance and cooled, then reheated as potato cakes. Put them on an oiled baking sheet and bake at 200°C/400°F/Gas Mark 6 for 20 minutes, until golden brown on top.

Mini potato fondants

These potatoes are awash with butter but a little richness goes a long way. At Braeval we use the little French 'mids' but any new potato about 5–6 cm (2–2½ in) in length will do. We usually allow 4 per portion but people invariably want more.

- 16–20 even-sized 'mids' new potatoes
- 175 g (6 oz) unsalted butter
- Maldon salt
- Freshly ground white pepper

SERVES FOUR

Pre-heat the oven to 190°/375°F/Gas Mark 5.

You need an ovenproof frying pan, preferably non-stick, which will hold all the potatoes in a single layer. First slice the tops and bottoms off the potatoes, which should leave you with unpeeled cylinders around 2.5 cm (1 in) high. Now cut the butter into strips about 3 mm (⅛ in) wide and line the base of the frying pan with them. Set the potatoes cut-face down on top of the butter to fill the pan. Season well. Put the frying pan over a low to medium heat and keep an eye on it as the butter melts. It should just bubble gently but don't allow it to get too hot or you'll burn the bottoms of the potatoes. They should be nicely browned after about 35–40 minutes, so then put them into the oven for 10–15 minutes, to cook. Take them out and let them stand in a warm place until you're ready to serve. They need about 10–20 minutes for the butter to be absorbed but will keep well for 1½ hours. To serve, lift them out of the pan, turn them over and place on the plate with the richly coloured side up.

STRAW POTATOES

Straw potatoes are thinner and crisper than your standard chips, and great with a peppered steak and some salad. The best varieties of potato are Golden Wonder, Kerr's Pink, Cyprus or even big Maris Piper bakers. I've also used sweet potatoes to good effect (see page 111). You really need a mandolin grater to get the right shape of chip. I use the medium blade on my Japanese mandolin. A wok is good for deep-frying the potatoes as its shape helps prevent the oil from boiling over.

450 g (1 lb) potatoes, peeled
Sunflower oil for deep-frying
Maldon salt
Freshly ground white pepper

SERVES FOUR

Use a mandolin to cut the potatoes into narrow strips about 3 mm (⅛ in) thick. Wash them in cold water, then put them in a clean tea towel and wring out as much moisture as you can. Pour 2.5 cm (1 in) of oil into a large deep saucepan or a wok and heat to 180°C/350°F (you could, of course, use a deep-fat fryer). Drop the potatoes into the hot oil a few at a time. Don't throw them all in at once or the oil will boil over. Fry them, stirring from time to time, until pale golden – this will take about 5–6 minutes. Drain on kitchen paper, season with salt and freshly ground white pepper and serve. You can keep these warm in a low oven for 30 minutes.

Seared potato slices

I came up with this one on *Ready Steady Cook*, a constant source of inspiration for quick, effective recipes. Use nice big baking potatoes for this, Maris Pipers if you can. You also need one of those heavy cast iron ribbed grill pans. This gives the potatoes a nice chargrilled flavour and they look good, too.

2 large baking potatoes, unpeeled, cut into slices 1 cm (1/2 in) thick
2 tablespoons olive oil
Maldon salt
Freshly ground white pepper

SERVES FOUR

Drop the potato slices into a large pan of boiling salted water and simmer for 8–10 minutes, or until almost tender. Meanwhile, heat the ribbed grill pan over a medium heat. When the potatoes are ready, remove them with a slotted spoon and pat dry on a tea towel. Brush them with some of the olive oil and season with salt and pepper. Place them on the pan and leave for 3–4 minutes. Then turn through a 90-degree angle and cook for another 3 minutes or so – this gives them an attractive criss-cross pattern. Brush again with plenty of oil, then turn over and cook as for the first side. That's them ready for a potato beauty contest.

PREVIOUS PAGES:
Top left: Mini Potato Fondants (see page 124)
Right: Straw Potatoes (see page 125)
Bottom left: Crushed Potatoes with Olive Oil, Parmesan and Basil (see page 124)

HONEY-GLAZED POTATOES AND PARSNIPS

This is based on the classic French boulangère potatoes. The inherent sweetness of the parsnips is picked up by the honey, and the result is a tasty layered side dish that doesn't overload on the richness. Try it as an accompaniment to game.

Pre-heat the oven to 200°C/400°F/Gas Mark 6.

Melt 50 g (2 oz) of the butter in a large saucepan. Add the onions and cook gently for about 5–6 minutes, until softened. Stir in the honey, lemon juice, stock and some seasoning and bring to the boil. Add the sliced potatoes and parsnips and check the seasoning. Spoon the mixture into a shallow ovenproof dish and press down lightly. Dot the top with the rest of the butter and cook for 45 minutes, until all the stock has been absorbed and the top is shiny and golden.

65 g (2½ oz) butter
2 onions, thinly sliced
2 tablespoons clear honey
1 teaspoon lemon juice
450 ml (15 fl oz) Chicken Stock (see page 170)
350 g (12 oz) large potatoes, thinly sliced
350 g (12 oz) parsnips, thinly sliced
Maldon salt
Freshly ground white pepper

SERVES EIGHT

VEGETABLE PURÉES

Most root vegetables make good purées. Celeriac is my favourite and, strangely, goes equally well with fish or game. The method for celeriac is given below. The basic principle, with a few adjustments, is the same for all the variations.

1 celeriac, weighing about 450 g (1 lb)
900 ml (1 1/2 pints) milk
50 g (2 oz) butter
Maldon salt
Freshly ground white pepper

SERVES EIGHT

Cut the top and bottom off the celeriac, then cut it into quarters. Use a small knife to peel it (take off slices about 5 mm (1/4 in) thick) and cut each quarter into 8 pieces. Put them in a saucepan and pour in the milk so that it just covers the celeriac. Season with salt and pepper and bring to the boil, then simmer very gently for 15–20 minutes, until the celeriac is very tender. Pour the contents of the pan into a sieve set over a bowl and reserve the cooking liquid. Put the hot celeriac in a food processor with the butter and about 4 tablespoons of the milk and purée for 3–4 minutes, until very smooth. Check the seasoning and then you're ready. This can be made the day before and gently reheated with a knob of butter.

VARIATIONS

CARROT: Use water instead of milk. Cook for 30–40 minutes, or until very tender and add a tablespoon of lemon juice to the cooking water.

BEETROOT: Wear rubber gloves to peel the beetroot, then cook it in water instead of milk for 45 minutes–1 hour.

SPINACH: Remove the stalks from 1.5 kg (3 lb) of spinach and cook slowly in a covered pan with 3–4 tablespoons of Nage (see page 168) for 15–20 minutes. Remove the lid towards the end of cooking to allow some of the liquid to evaporate.

Salad of Herbs

This turns up everywhere in my restaurant and is probably my favourite garnish of the moment. The fresh flavours of the herbs are far better than boring salad leaves. The secret is to divide the herbs into nice sprigs and keep them in a mixing bowl covered in clingfilm in the fridge until you are ready to add the dressing. But do serve them the second the dressing goes on as they lose their texture and colour rapidly. You can vary the herbs to suit each dish but I always return to the following combinations: basil, flatleaf parsley and rocket; chervil, tarragon and fennel; and chives, dill and chervil.

25 g (1 oz) mixed fresh herbs
1 tablespoon olive oil
1 teaspoon lemon juice
Maldon salt
Freshly ground white pepper

Season the herbs with a pinch of salt and 4 turns of the white pepper mill. Drizzle over the oil, add the lemon juice and gently toss the leaves to coat. Divide into 4 neat piles to serve, and that's it.

SERVES FOUR

Deep-fried Herbs

Deep-fried herbs are very trendy at the moment. Quite rightly, since deep-frying improves the texture of the herbs and concentrates the flavour. You can use any herbs you like, but my favourites are flatleaf and curly parsley, sage, rocket, basil, tarragon and chives. Chervil, however, tends to go a bit gooey. This also works for celery leaves.

Fresh herbs
Sunflower oil for deep-frying
Maldon salt

Divide the herbs into large sprigs but not down to individual leaves. Have ready a plate lined with a double layer of kitchen paper on which to drain the herbs. Heat the oil to 180°C/350°F; it shouldn't be too hot. Drop the herbs into the oil in 2 batches and turn with a slotted spoon during cooking. They are ready once they stop sizzling, which shouldn't take more than 2 minutes. Drain and season with a tiny amount of salt.

Herb tempura

A dramatic-looking and very tasty garnish. The best herbs to use are chives, parsley, basil, rocket, tarragon and coriander.

15 g (1/2 oz) fresh herbs
1/2 quantity of Tempura Batter (see page 29)
Sunflower oil for deep-frying
Maldon salt
Freshly ground white pepper

SERVES FOUR

Heat the oil to 180°C/350°F. Pick the herbs over but don't remove the stalks. Dip them in the batter 2 or 3 at a time and then drop them in the hot oil. Don't crowd the pan. Turn after 1 minute and then remove with a slotted spoon as soon as they are pale golden brown. Drain on kitchen paper and serve immediately.

PART NINE

PUDDINGS

Carragheen pudding with boozy blaeberries

There are still many surprise pleasures to be found at the beach. Carragheen seaweed is the setting agent in this blancmange-style pudding. It was traditionally used as a restorative on the Isle of Skye so I was expecting an unpleasant medicinal taste. But after trying it I can vouch for its rightful presence in the modern kitchen. If you can't gather your own, buy it dried and follow the packet instructions for use. This dish looks like an exotic mixture but both the primary ingredients were actually found almost side by side at the shore. Blueberries would do instead of blaeberries.

65 g (2½ oz) fresh or 20g (¾ oz) dried carragheen
600 ml (1 pint) milk
65 g (2½ oz) caster sugar

FOR THE BLAEBERRIES:
150 ml (5 fl oz) water
150 g (5 oz) caster sugar
175–225 g (6–8 oz) blaeberries
2 tablespoons gin

SERVES FOUR

If using fresh carragheen, leave in a tray in a sunny position for 2–3 days or bake overnight on a low heat in the oven to dry it out. When ready to prepare the pudding, soak the carragheen in plenty of warm water for 10 minutes, then drain and squeeze dry. Pour the milk into a pan, add the carragheen and bring to a simmer. Simmer for 5 minutes, or until the mixture becomes gelatinous and thick. Pour into a sieve set over a large jug or bowl and leave to drain. You may have to work the milky mixture through gently with a wooden spoon. Whisk in the sugar and then pour the mixture into four 85 ml (3 fl oz) dariole moulds. Leave to set in the fridge, preferably overnight.

For the blaeberries, put the water and sugar into a pan and leave over a low heat until the sugar has completely dissolved. Bring to the boil and boil for 5 minutes. Add the blaeberries and gin, bring back to the boil, then tip into a bowl and leave to cool. Leave in the fridge overnight.

To serve, dip the dariole moulds into hot water for a few seconds to release the puddings. Unmould into the centre of each serving plate and spoon around the blaeberries and gin syrup.

Vanilla Ice-Cream with Deep-Fried Fruit Cheese

Ice-cream should be delicately flavoured and velvety smooth and should really be churned and eaten on the same day.

600 ml (1 pint) milk
2 split vanilla pods
6 medium egg yolks
75 g (3 oz) caster sugar
250 ml (8 fl oz) double cream

FOR THE DEEP-FRIED FRUIT CHEESE:

75 g (3oz) fruit cheese
Sunflower oil for deep-frying
100 g (4 oz) plain flour
25 g (1 oz) caster sugar, plus extra for dredging
150 ml (5 fl oz) lager-style beer

SERVES SIX

Put the milk and the vanilla pods into a pan and bring slowly to the boil. Take off the heat and leave for 20 minutes to allow the flavour of the vanilla to infuse.

Whisk the egg yolks and sugar together in a bowl until pale and creamy. Bring the milk back to the boil, lift out the pods and whisk the milk into the egg yolks. Return the mixture to the pan and cook over a gentle heat, stirring constantly, until it thickens enough to coat the back of the wooden spoon lightly. It shouldn't take more than 3 minutes. Stir in the double cream and leave to cool. Cover and place in the fridge until well chilled. Now you can either churn the mixture in an ice-cream maker or pour it into a shallow plastic box and freeze until almost firm. Scrape the mixture into a food processor and whizz until smooth. Pour it back into the box and repeat once more. Return the ice-cream to the freezer and freeze until firm.

If the ice-cream has been made in advance, transfer it from the freezer to the fridge about 30 minutes before serving to allow it time to soften slightly.

For the fruit cheese, cut the cheese into 1 x 2 cm (1/2 x 3/4 in) blocks. Heat some oil for deep-frying to 180°C/350°F. Sift the flour and sugar into a bowl and whisk in the beer until smooth. Dip the fruit cheese pieces into the batter and deep-fry a few pieces at a time until crisp and golden. Drain on kitchen paper, dust with caster sugar and serve with the ice-cream.

VARIATION

Make the ice-cream as above, substituting 1 1/2 lightly crushed cinnamon sticks for the pods. Whisk the yolks with 65 g (2 1/2 oz) sugar, and stir in only 100 ml (4 fl oz) double cream before freezing. Serve with Cherry and Almond Tart (see page 156).

Honey and Whisky Ice-cream

Use a good sherry-cask-matured malt like a Macallan 10 and you'll end up with the silkiest, sexiest ice-cream this side of a freezer full of Häagen-Dazs. It's basically a hot toddy that thinks it's a pudding and is marvellous with Mincemeat Tart (see page 161).

600 ml (1 pint) milk
6 medium egg yolks
25 g (1 oz) caster sugar
150 g (5 oz) heather honey
50 ml (2 fl oz) whisky
85 ml (3 fl oz) double cream

SERVES SIX

Pour the milk into a pan and bring to the boil. Meanwhile, whisk the egg yolks and sugar together in a bowl until pale and creamy. Whisk in the hot milk, return the mixture to the pan and cook over a gentle heat, stirring constantly, until it thickens enough to coat the back of the wooden spoon lightly. Pour the mixture into a bowl and stir in the honey, whisky and double cream. Leave until cold and then cover and place in the fridge until well chilled. Proceed as for the Cinnamon Ice-cream (see page 135).

Wild Strawberry Ice-cream in Brandy Snap Baskets

There is no better place to eat wild fruit than out in the open, but this ice-cream would be a nice final resting place for any you do bring home. Small wild strawberries grow widely in early summer and, though they may be quite labour intensive to pick, the intense flavour of the dark, ripe fruit will be well worth it.

Home-made ice-cream is always a big hit and if you have an ice-cream maker all you have to do is bung in the correct ingredients at the correct time. This is a coarse ice-cream, with plenty of strawberry pieces running through it.

600 ml (1 pint) milk
6 medium egg yolks
75 g (3 oz) caster sugar
100 g (4 oz) wild strawberries

FOR THE BRANDY SNAPS:

25 g (1 oz) butter
25 g (1 oz) caster sugar
25 g (1 oz) golden syrup
25 g (1 oz) plain flour

FOR THE STRAWBERRY SAUCE:

100 g (4 oz) wild strawberries
50 ml (2 fl oz) Stock Syrup (see page 187)

SERVES FOUR

For the ice-cream, bring the milk to the boil in a saucepan. Meanwhile, whisk the egg yolks and sugar together in a bowl until pale and creamy. Pour the boiling milk onto the egg yolks and whisk away. Return the mixture to the pan and cook over a gentle heat for a few minutes, stirring constantly, until it thickens enough to coat the back of the wooden spoon lightly. Remove from the heat, pour into a bowl and leave to cool. Then leave in the fridge until really cold. Now either churn in an ice-cream maker, adding the strawberries half way through churning, or freeze by hand, stirring in the strawberries after giving it its last whizz in the food processor (see Vanilla Ice-cream on page 135).

For the brandy snaps, melt the butter, sugar and golden syrup together, then beat in the flour. Leave to mixture to cool and then chill it in the fridge until firm. Now scoop it onto a large sheet of clingfilm and shape into a roll 2.5 cm (1 in) thick. Wrap firmly in the clingfilm and chill once more until really hard.

Pre-heat the oven to 200 °C/400°F/Gas Mark 6.

Cut 4 slices 5 mm (1/4 in) thick off the roll and place them well spaced apart on a lightly oiled baking sheet. Return the roll to the fridge or it will go soft again. (The mixture keeps well, refrigerated, for a week or freezes well and any leftover cooked brandy snaps keep well in an airtight tin.) Bake for 5 minutes or until richly golden. Remove from the oven and leave on the baking sheet for 1 minute. Then lift off with a palette knife and and drape each one over an upturned egg cup to form a little basket. Remove when set.

For the sauce, work the strawberries through a sieve with the back of a ladle and add the stock syrup.

If you have made the ice-cream some time in advance, transfer it from the freezer to the fridge about 30 minutes before serving to allow it to soften slightly.

To serve, place a scoop of ice-cream in each brandy snap basket and drizzle the sauce around.

ALMOND AND CHOC CHIP CAKE WITH RICARD ICE-CREAM

The anise flavour of the Ricard and the almond biscuits complement each other very well. Pernod could be substituted if you can't get Ricard.

10 amaretti biscuits
75 g (3 oz) good-quality plain chocolate (65% cocoa solids)
100 g (4 oz) self-raising flour
225 g (8 oz) unsalted butter, softened
225 g (8 oz) caster sugar
5 medium eggs, separated
Icing sugar for dusting

FOR THE RICARD ICE-CREAM:

250 ml (8 fl oz) double cream
250 ml (8 fl oz) milk
1 teaspoon instant espresso coffee granules
3 star anise
6 medium egg yolks
100 g (4 oz) caster sugar
50 ml (2 fl oz) Ricard

SERVES EIGHT

First make the ice-cream. Bring the cream, milk and espresso granules to the boil in a pan. Add the star anise and set aside for 20 minutes to allow the flavour to infuse the milk. Whisk the egg yolks and sugar together in a bowl until creamy. Bring the cream and milk back to the boil, remove the star anise and then whisk into the yolks. Return the mixture to the pan and cook over a gentle heat for a few minutes, stirring constantly, until it thickens enough to coat the back of the wooden spoon lightly. Pour the mixture into a bowl and leave to cool, then stir in the Ricard and set aside in the fridge until well chilled. Now you can either churn the mixture in an ice-cream maker or freeze by hand (see Cinnamon Ice-cream on page 135).

Pre-heat the oven to 160°C/325°F/Gas Mark 3. Grease a 25 cm (10 in) springform tin with a little butter and then line the base with silicone paper.

Break the amaretti into a food processor and grind them to a fine powder (alternatively, seal them in a plastic bag and crush with a rolling pin). Chop the chocolate into chips. Put the crushed biscuits and chopped chocolate into a bowl with 75 g (3 oz) of the flour.

Beat the butter and sugar together until pale and fluffy. Beat in the rest of the flour and then the egg yolks, one at a time. Gently fold in the biscuit and flour mixture.

Whisk the egg whites in a separate bowl until they form soft peaks – the tips of the peaks should fold over, not stand upright. Gently fold them into the cake mixture and then spoon it into the prepared tin and bake for 1 hour, or until a fine skewer inserted into the centre comes out clean. Leave the cake in the tin on a wire rack to cool.

If you have made your ice-cream some time in advance, transfer it from the freezer to the fridge about 30 minutes before serving to allow it time to soften slightly.

Remove the cake from the tin and carefully peel off the lining paper. Cut into 8 wedges, dust with icing sugar and serve with the ice-cream.

Passion Fruit Tart with Pineapple and Lime Sorbet

This is similar to lemon tart but the passion fruit adds fragrance as well as zing. It should be crisp and caramelised on the outside, sweet, smooth and zesty on the inside.

- 1 quantity Sweet Flan Pastry (see page 186)
- 6 medium eggs
- 275 g (10 oz) caster sugar
- 300 ml (10 fl oz) passion fruit coulis or juice (see page 152)
- 300 ml (10 fl oz) double cream
- Icing sugar for dusting

FOR THE PINEAPPLE AND LIME SORBET:

- 1 ripe pineapple
- Juice and finely grated zest of 2 limes
- 250 ml (8 fl oz) Stock Syrup (see page 187)

SERVES EIGHT

Use the pastry to line a 25 cm (20 in) flan ring and bake it blind as described on page 186.

For the pineapple and lime sorbet, slice the top and the bottom off the pineapple and carefully cut away all the peel and the little black 'eyes'. Cut the fruit into quarters, remove the core and roughly chop the flesh. Put the pineapple flesh, lime juice and zest and sugar syrup into a food processor and whizz until smooth. Now you can either churn the mixture in an ice-cream maker or freeze it by hand (see Cinnamon Ice-cream on page 135).

For the tart, pre-heat the oven to 150°C/300°F/ Gas Mark 2.

Gently whisk the eggs with the sugar until smooth. Whisk in the passion fruit coulis and then stir in the double cream – don't do this too vigorously as you don't want to create too many bubbles in the mixture. Lift any froth off the top of the mixture and then pour it into the blind-baked flan case. Bake in the oven for 25 minutes or until just set.

Remove the tart from the oven and leave to cool for about 30 minutes. Once cool, cut into 8 portions but leave it in its original shape. Now pre-heat the grill to its highest setting. Heavily dredge each slice with icing sugar, slide them as near to the heat as you can and leave until the sugar has caramelised. However, if you have a blowtorch, you can use this instead to caramelise the sugar. Leave to cool slightly once more, then serve with a scoop of the pineapple and lime sorbet.

Chocolate Orange Cheesecake

Not surprisingly, the inspiration for this came from eating a Terry's Chocolate Orange. It's made with easily accessible ingredients. To save time, you could omit one of the sauces, though the ones I've included work nicely together.

3 oranges
50 g (2 oz) butter, melted
1/2 teaspoon ground mixed spice
1/2 teaspoon ground cinnamon
100 g (4 oz) digestive biscuits, crushed
225 g (8 oz) good-quality plain chocolate (65% cocoa solids)
100 g (4 oz) caster sugar plus 2 teaspoons
120 ml (4 fl oz) water
225 g (8 oz) full-fat cream cheese
150 ml (5 fl oz) double cream
3 tablespoons brandy
1 teaspoon cornflour
3 tablespoons milk
1 tablespoon cocoa powder

SERVES FOUR

Finely grate the zest from half of 1 orange. Place all but 1 tablespoon of the melted butter into a bowl with the mixed spice, cinnamon, crushed biscuits and orange zest and mix together well. Place four 10 cm (4 in) scone cutters on a baking sheet. Divide the crumbs between the rings and press them down lightly. Brush the sides of the rings with the rest of the melted butter.

Break the chocolate into a bowl and rest over a pan of barely simmering water. Leave until melted, then remove the pan from the heat and set aside.

Pare the zest from the 2 remaining oranges with a potato peeler, taking care not the remove any of the bitter white pith underneath. Cut the strips into very fine needleshreds. Put the 100 g (4 oz) of caster sugar into a pan with the water and leave over a gentle heat until the sugar has completely dissolved. Bring to the boil, add the orange needleshreds and simmer for 10 minutes.

Meanwhile, put the cream cheese into a bowl and whisk until smooth. Beat in half the melted chocolate (the rest will be made into a chocolate sauce). Pour the cream into another bowl and whip until it begins to form soft peaks. Whisk in 2 tablespoons of the brandy and 1 teaspoon of the remaining sugar. Gently fold into the cream cheese mixture and then spoon it into the metal rings. Place in the freezer for 15 minutes or in the fridge until firm.

Strain the orange syrup through a sieve into a bowl, reserving the shreds of zest. Squeeze the juice from 2 of the oranges and place in a small pan with the cornflour. Bring to the boil, whisking all the time and simmer for 1 minute until thickened. Stir in 2 tablespoons of the orange syrup (you can either discard the remainder or store it in a jar in the fridge for another occasion). Spread the orange needleshreds over a plate and sprinkle with the remaining teaspoon of caster sugar and toss lightly until they become well coated.

Stir the milk and the rest of the brandy into the remaining melted chocolate. Now, if you like, cut all the peel and white pith off the last orange and remove the flesh in segments by cutting either side of each membrane.

To serve, remove the cheesecakes from the fridge and transfer each one to a plate using a palette knife. Briefly warm the outside of each ring with a warm, wet cloth and remove. Dust the top of each one with the cocoa powder through a fine sieve and then pile the orange needleshreds on top. Drizzle the orange and chocolate sauces around each cheesecake and decorate the plate with the orange segments, if you like.

OVERLEAF:
Left: Chocolate Orange Cheesecake (see above)
Right: Soft Chocolate Cake with Mascarpone Cream and Espresso Coffee Sauce (see page 144)

SOFT CHOCOLATE CAKE WITH MASCARPONE CREAM AND ESPRESSO COFFEE SAUCE

You might as well ask me to list the moons of Jupiter as name my favourite pudding. This one comes close, though. It's as rich and moist as any chocolate cake I've ever tasted. Coffee and cream have a special affinity, and all these ingredients sit well together. I use espresso coffee as much for its aroma as its flavour. The mascarpone cream could be replaced with ordinary whipped cream or chocolate sauce.

225 g (8 oz) good-quality plain chocolate (65% cocoa solids)
225 g (8 oz) unsalted butter
150 g (5 oz) caster sugar
6 medium egg yolks
8 medium egg whites
Icing sugar, sifted, to decorate

FOR THE MASCARPONE CREAM:

175 g (6 oz) mascarpone
25 g (1 oz) caster sugar
50 ml (2 fl oz) double cream

FOR THE ESPRESSO COFFEE SAUCE:

6 egg yolks
75 g (3 oz) caster sugar
600 ml (1 pint) milk
50 ml (2 fl oz) extra strong espresso coffee or 1 teaspoon espresso granules dissolved in 50 ml (2 fl oz) hot water
2 tablespoons Kahlua liqueur

Pre-heat the oven to 160°C/325°F/Gas Mark 3. Lightly butter a 25 cm (10 in) springform cake tin and then line the base with a circle of silicone paper.

Break the chocolate into a bowl and add the butter. Rest over a pan of simmering water, making sure that the bowl does not touch the water. Leave to melt, stirring until it is smooth. Remove and set aside.

Put the sugar and egg yolks into a large bowl and whisk together until the mixture becomes pale and thick and leaves a trail on the surface for a few seconds. Gently fold this into the melted chocolate.

Now whisk the egg whites into soft peaks – the tips of the peaks should just fold over, not stand upright. Very gently fold the whites into the chocolate mixture. Pour into the tin and bake for 45 minutes. It will soufflé up during cooking and just crack when it's ready but then collapse once you bring it out of the oven. Don't worry; this is just the way it should be. Leave to cool in the tin.

For the mascarpone cream, beat the mascarpone and caster sugar together until smooth, then gradually whisk in the double cream. Cover and chill until needed.

For the coffee sauce, whisk the egg yolks and sugar together in a bowl until thick and creamy. Bring the milk to the boil in a small pan, then whisk it into the egg yolks. Pour the mixture back into the pan and cook over a gentle heat, stirring constantly, until it is thick enough to coat the back of the wooden spoon lightly. Stir in the coffee and the liqueur and leave to cool. Cover and chill until required. For the caramel twists, heat the sugar and water in a pan over a low heat until clear. Boil rapidly until it turns dark. Plunge the base of the pan into cold water to arrest cooking and quickly drizzle tight swirls of caramel from a spoon onto a foil-lined baking sheet. Leave to set.

Carefully remove the cake from the tin and peel off the paper. Cut the cake into wedges and place on serving plates. Dredge with icing sugar and push a twist into the top of each wedge. Serve with a spoonful of the mascarpone cream and pour the espresso sauce around. Alternatively, use a dark chocolate sauce and drizzle it with the coffee sauce to make an attractive pattern.

FOR THE CARAMEL TWISTS:

100 g (4 oz) granulated sugar
25 ml (1 fl oz) water

SERVES EIGHT

Cinnamon Cream with Spiced Rhubarb

This cinnamon cream is really just *panna cotta* (an Italian set cream), flavoured with cinnamon instead of vanilla. We serve it in early summer when the first pale-pink forced rhubarb arrives. If you're using the later, main-crop rhubarb, increase the cooking time a little. It's direct, simple and unfussy, and can be made well in advance.

750 ml (1 1/4 pints) double cream
1 cinnamon stick
1/2 teaspoon ground cinnamon
3 gelatine leaves
75 g (3 oz) caster sugar

FOR THE SPICED RHUBARB:

750 g (1 1/2 lb) rhubarb
450 ml (15 fl oz) water

Put the cream, cinnamon stick and ground cinnamon into a pan and bring to the boil. Remove from the heat and leave to stand for about 20 minutes to allow the flavour of the cinnamon to infuse the cream. Meanwhile, soak the gelatine leaves in cold water for 10 minutes. Remove the cinnamon stick from the pan and bring the cream to just below boiling point once more. Add the caster sugar and the soaked gelatine and stir until they have both dissolved. Strain the mixture into a jug and then pour it into eight 85 ml (3 fl oz) dariole moulds. Leave overnight in the fridge to set.

425 g (15 oz) granulated sugar
1 cinnamon stick
3 star anise
6 cloves
1 vanilla pod
A strip of pared lemon zest

SERVES EIGHT

For the spiced rhubarb, cut the rhubarb into 4 cm (1½ in) lengths (if you are using main-crop rhubarb, you may need to peel it first). Put the water and sugar in a large pan and bring slowly to the boil, stirring now and then until the sugar has dissolved. Add the spices, vanilla pod and strip of lemon zest and simmer for 5 minutes. Add the rhubarb, bring back to the boil and simmer gently for 2 minutes (slightly longer if you are using older rhubarb). Set aside and leave to cool. Leave the spices, vanilla pod and lemon zest in the syrup to allow the flavours to develop.

To serve, dip the dariole moulds very briefly into warm water and then unmould them onto dessert plates. Spoon the rhubarb alongside.

LAYERED WHITE AND DARK CHOCOLATE MOUSSE

You can either serve these mousses layered up in tall glasses or sandwich them together between discs of tempered plain chocolate. These stacks would be great served with a fresh raspberry coulis, some Crème Anglaise (see page 164) and fresh raspberries.

FOR THE DARK CHOCOLATE MOUSSE:

165 g (5½ oz) good-quality plain chocolate (65% cocoa solids)
3 medium egg yolks
5 medium egg whites
50 g (2 oz) caster sugar

If you are making chocolate discs, you will need to do them first. To temper the chocolate, break 200 g (7 oz) of it into a bowl and place over a pan of barely simmering water, making sure that the bowl is not touching the water. Leave over a low heat until melted. Then take the bowl off the pan, break the remaining chocolate into small pieces and stir it in until it melts. Depending on the temperature of your kitchen (you need it to be cool), lightly oil either a smooth work surface or a large, chilled baking sheet. Cover with a large sheet of clingfilm, pour on the chocolate and spread it out in a thin layer with a palette knife. Leave to cool, or put it in the fridge, until set. You can now cut the chocolate into 7.5 cm

(3 in) discs using a plain pastry cutter or cut them into squares with a knife. Lift them off the clingfilm (they will pop off quite easily) and set aside, in a single layer, somewhere cool until needed.

For the dark chocolate mousse, break the chocolate into a bowl and melt as for the chocolate discs. Take the bowl off the pan and leave to cool slightly if it gets a little too warm. Then beat in the egg yolks until the mixture is smooth and coming away from the sides of the bowl. In a large bowl whisk the egg whites into soft peak – the tips of the peaks should just flip over, not stand upright. Gradually whisk in the sugar, making sure that the mixture doesn't get too stiff. Stir a quarter of the egg whites into the chocolate to loosen the mixture slightly, then gently fold in the remainder. Refrigerate while you make the white chocolate mousse.

For the white chocolate mousse, rest a bowl over a pan of barely simmering water until it is warm. Break the white chocolate into the bowl, take the pan off the heat immediately and set aside until the chocolate has melted – it is very important not to let white chocolate get too hot or it will go grainy and it is then very difficult to work with. Meanwhile, soak the gelatine leaf in cold water for 10 minutes. Take the bowl of chocolate off the pan and beat in the soaked gelatine and the egg yolks. The mixture will look as if it has split at first but just keep beating it and it will come back together and go smooth. In 2 separate bowls, whisk the cream and the egg whites into soft peaks. Fold the cream into the chocolate mixture, followed by the egg whites.

You can now either alternate layers of dark and white chocolate mousse in 8 tall glasses and chill overnight, or cover the 2 bowls and chill overnight. Then, to serve, place a disc or square of chocolate on each plate and top with a spoonful of dark chocolate mousse. Cover with another piece of chocolate and then some white chocolate mousse. Top with a final layer of chocolate and dust with icing sugar.

FOR THE WHITE CHOCOLATE MOUSSE:

175 g (6 oz) good-quality white chocolate
1 gelatine leaf
2 medium egg yolks
250 ml (8 fl oz) double cream
2 medium egg whites

FOR THE CHOCOLATE DISCS (OPTIONAL):

300 g (11 oz) good-quality plain chocolate (65% cocoa solids)

SERVES EIGHT

Caramelised Rice Pudding with a Compote of Blueberries

A light, unusual pudding with an impressive, crunchy, caramelised top, this tastes twenty times better than it sounds and bears no resemblance at all to school dinners. The blueberries need poaching to bring out the flavours. Their deep colour contrasts nicely with the neutral shade of the rice pudding.

1 vanilla pod, split
600 ml (1 pint) milk
65 g (2½ oz) caster sugar
50 g (2 oz) pudding rice
120 ml (4 fl oz) double cream
Icing sugar for dusting

FOR THE COMPOTE:

250 ml (8 fl oz) Stock Syrup (see page 187)
Juice of ½ lemon
1 tablespoon crème de myrtilles or cassis, optional
225 g (8 oz) blueberries

SERVES FOUR

For the rice pudding, put the split vanilla pod, milk and sugar into a pan and bring slowly to the boil. Stir in the rice, bring back to the boil and simmer very gently for about 1 hour, until thick and gooey. Take off the heat, leave to cool and then chill.

For the compote, bring the sugar syrup, lemon juice and crème de myrtilles or cassis, if using, to the boil in a pan. Add the blueberries and simmer for 2 minutes, then pour into a bowl and leave to cool.

To finish off the rice pudding, whip the double cream until it forms soft peaks and fold it lightly into the cooled rice mixture. Place a deep 6 cm (2½ in) scone cutter on a baking sheet. Spoon in the rice mixture, lightly level the top and then remove the cutter and repeat three times. Dust heavily with icing sugar. Caramelise the sugar either with a blowtorch or by putting the baking sheet under a very hot grill until the sugar is bubbling and has turned a dark golden brown. Set aside and leave to cool slightly. Then slide a fish slice under each pudding and transfer to a dessert plate. Spoon some of the blueberry compote around and serve.

Caramel Mousse Brûlée

This is just one of the many great puddings originated by my friend Jim Kerr, formerly of the Rogano restaurant in Glasgow. It's actually quite a light pudding that has all the flavour of caramel without any of the sticky sweetness.

150 g (5 oz) granulated sugar
1/2 vanilla pod, split open
85 ml (3 fl oz) water
2 gelatine leaves
5 medium eggs
1 1/2 tablespoons caster sugar
300 ml (10 fl oz) double cream
Icing sugar for dusting

TO SERVE:

8 scoops Caramel Ice-cream (see page 153)
8 Tuile Cones (see page 188)

SERVES EIGHT

To make the caramel, put the granulated sugar, vanilla pod and half the water into a heavy-based pan. Leave over a low heat until the sugar has completely dissolved and the liquid is clear. Increase the heat and boil until the liquid turns a very dark caramel colour. Quickly remove the pan from the heat, stand back and add the remaining water – it will hiss and splutter alarmingly but don't worry. Return the pan to a low heat until all the hardened pieces of caramel have dissolved. Meanwhile, soak the gelatine leaves in cold water for 5–10 minutes. Take the caramel off the heat and leave to cool for 2 minutes. Add the soaked gelatine and stir gently until dissolved.

Meanwhile, separate the eggs into 2 large, clean bowls. Add the caster sugar to the yolks and whisk with an electric beater until the mixture is very pale and thick – it should leave a visible trail for a few seconds. Pour in the caramel, whisking constantly, then whisk for another 3 minutes.

Whisk the egg whites into soft peaks – the tips of the peaks should just flip over, not stand upright. Whip the double cream softly. Gently fold the egg whites into the caramel mixture, followed by the cream. Pour the mousse into eight 7.5 cm (3 in) ramekins, making sure it comes right up to the rim as they sink a tad as they start to set. Leave overnight in the fridge.

To serve, dust the tops of the mousses heavily with icing sugar. Heat several long skewers in a gas flame until red hot and rest them lightly on the sugar to brand it in a criss-cross pattern. Drop small scoops of the ice-cream into the tuile cones and serve alongside.

OVERLEAF:
Left: Caramelised Rice Pudding with a Compote of Blueberries (see opposite)
Right: Caramel Mousse Brûlée (see above)

Passion fruit délice

This can be made up three or four days in advance and is easy to serve as a lovely fresh end to a meal. I use ready-made French passion fruit coulis which saves so much time, but if you can't get hold of any you will need to use 36 passion fruit. Halve them and scoop out the pulp into a sieve set over a bowl. Work out the juice with a wooden spoon and discard the seeds.

450 ml (15 fl oz) milk
1/2 vanilla pod
6 medium egg yolks
120 g (4 1/2 oz) caster sugar
4 1/2 gelatine leaves
300 ml (10 fl oz) passion fruit coulis or juice
450 ml (15 fl oz) double cream

FOR THE JELLY GLAZE:

1 gelatine leaf
120 ml (4 fl oz) passion fruit coulis or juice
85 ml (3 fl oz) Stock Syrup (see page 187)

SERVES TEN

Put the milk and vanilla pod in a pan and bring to the boil. Meanwhile, whisk the egg yolks and sugar together in a bowl until pale and creamy. Lift out the vanilla pod and whisk the milk into the egg yolks. Pour the mixture back into the pan and cook over a gentle heat, stirring constantly, until the mixture thickens enough to coat the back of the wooden spoon lightly. Set aside.

Soak the gelatine leaves in cold water for 10 minutes. Pour the passion fruit coulis into a pan and warm through over a low heat, then add the soaked gelatine and stir until dissolved. Leave to cool slightly and then stir this mixture into the custard. You can now do one of two things – either leave the mixture in the fridge for 3–4 hours until it begins to show signs of setting (and if you forget it, give it a good blitz with a hand mixer) or rest the bowl in a larger bowl containing some ice cubes and water and stir constantly until it starts to thicken. Lightly whip the cream into soft peaks and fold it in. Pour the mixture into ten 7.5 cm (3 in) ramekins or a 1.2 litre (2 pint) soufflé dish, leaving a little space at the top for the jelly glaze, and chill until set.

When the custard bases have set, make the glaze. Soak the gelatine leaf in cold water for 10 minutes. Pour the passion fruit coulis and sugar syrup into a pan and warm through over a gentle heat. Add the soaked gelatine and stir until it has dissolved. Pour a thin layer onto the top of each ramekin and chill once more until set.

Hot Caramel Soufflés with Caramel Ice-cream

First, a note of care with the caramel. Too dark is too bitter, too pale is too sweet. Get that right and you deserve a drumroll. The beautiful texture and spot-on aroma make this my favourite soufflé, be it savoury or sweet. Slide a couple of scoops of the ice-cream through a slit in the top of each soufflé for a lovely contrast in temperature and texture.

300 ml (10 fl oz) milk
3 medium egg yolks
315 g (11½ oz) caster sugar, plus extra for dusting
15 g (½ oz) cornflour
15 g (½ oz) plain flour
85 ml (3 fl oz) water
5 medium egg whites

FOR THE CARAMEL ICE-CREAM:
150 g (5 oz) caster sugar
40 ml (1½ fl oz) water
600 ml (1 pint) milk
6 medium egg yolks

SERVES SIX

First make the ice-cream. Put 100 g (4 oz) of the caster sugar into a large heavy-based pan and cook over a medium heat, stirring from time to time, until it has dissolved and cooked to a dark brown caramel. Take the pan off the heat, stand back and add the water. It will hiss and splutter alarmingly so be careful. Return to a low heat and stir until any pieces of hardened caramel have dissolved. Set aside and leave until cool, but not set.

Bring the milk to the boil in a saucepan. Whisk the egg yolks and remaining caster sugar together in a bowl until pale and creamy, then whisk in the hot milk. Return the mixture to the pan and cook over a gentle heat, stirring constantly, until it is thick enough to coat the back of the wooden spoon lightly. Stir in the cool caramel, strain the mixture into a bowl and leave to cool. Cover and chill well, then freeze as for Cinnamon Ice-cream (see page 135).

For the soufflés, pre-heat the oven to 220°C/425°F/Gas Mark 7.

If you have made the ice-cream some time in advance, transfer it from the freezer to the fridge about 30 minutes before serving to allow it to soften slightly.

Lightly butter six 7.5 cm (3 in) ramekins and then dust with some caster sugar. Set aside in the fridge.

Pour the milk into a pan and bring to the boil. Meanwhile, beat the egg yolks, 40 g (1½ oz) of the caster sugar, the cornflour and plain flour together in a bowl until smooth. Whisk in the hot milk, return the mixture to the pan and bring back to the boil, stirring. Reduce the heat and simmer gently for about 10 minutes to cook the flour through, then pour into a large mixing bowl and set aside.

Meanwhile, put the remaining caster sugar into a large heavy-based pan and cook to a dark brown caramel as for the ice-cream. Take the pan off the heat, add the water and then return to a low heat until smooth. Beat half the liquid caramel into the custard base and set aside.

Whisk the egg whites in a large bowl until they just begin to form peaks. Very gradually pour the remaining hot caramel into the egg whites in a slow steady stream, whisking all the time, until you have a stiff, glossy, caramel-coloured meringue. Now whisk one quarter of the meringue into the custard base, then very gently fold in the remainder. Spoon the mixture into the prepared ramekin dishes and cook for 12–13 minutes.

The soufflés should be well risen, browned and doubled in height but still slightly wobbly. Don't take them out too soon but don't be afraid to open the oven door to check them after the first 5 minutes.

Serve immediately, with the ice-cream.

APPLE SOUFFLÉS WITH APPLE SORBET

There are two very different flavours at work here. The intense, cooked flavour of the soufflé and the light zing of the sorbet.

The apple sorbet is one of the easiest puddings you'll ever have to make, and probably the cleverest. Leave the skins on the Granny Smiths and it will have a lovely pastel colour.

First make the apple sorbet. Toss the apple pieces in 1 tablespoon of the lemon juice and then spread them over a baking tray and freeze for about 1–1½ hours, until hard. Remove from the freezer and leave them to thaw slightly at room temperature for 10 minutes. Then scrape them into a food processor, add the remaining lemon juice and the stock syrup and process until smooth. Transfer the mixture to a plastic box, cover and freeze for 3–4 hours until firm.

For the apple soufflés, put the diced apples, cider and Calvados into a pan and cook over a low heat for about 30 minutes, beating with a wooden spoon now and then if necessary, until most of the liquid has evaporated and you are left with a very thick purée. Set aside.

Pre-heat the oven to 220°C/425°F/Gas Mark 7.

Lightly butter six 7.5 cm (3 in) ramekins, dust with a little caster sugar and set aside in the fridge. If you have made your sorbet some time beforehand, transfer it from the freezer to the fridge to soften slightly.

Bring the milk to the boil in a pan. Meanwhile, beat the egg yolks, 40 g (1½ oz) of the caster sugar, the cornflour and plain flour together in a bowl until smooth. Whisk in the hot milk, then return the mixture to the pan and bring back to the boil, stirring. Reduce the heat and simmer gently for about 10 minutes. Pour into a large mixing bowl and stir in the apple purée.

Whisk the egg whites to soft peaks, then very gradually whisk in the remaining caster sugar to make a soft meringue. Stir a quarter of the meringue into the apple custard to loosen the mixture slightly, then very gently fold in the remainder. Spoon the mixture into the prepared ramekins and bake for 12–13 minutes until brown but still slightly wobbly. The mixture won't double in height because of the extra weight of the apple. Serve immediately, with a scoop of the apple sorbet.

The sorbet also keeps well in the freezer for up to 2 weeks. Leave in the fridge for 10 minutes before eating.

4 Cox's apples, peeled, cored and diced
120 ml (4 fl oz) cider
2 tablespoons Calvados
300 ml (10 fl oz) milk
3 medium egg yolks
65 g (2½ oz) caster sugar, plus extra for dusting
15 g (½ oz) cornflour
15 g (½ oz) plain flour
4 medium egg whites

FOR THE APPLE SORBET:

4 Granny Smith apples, cored and diced
Juice of 1 lemon
85 ml (3 fl oz) Stock Syrup (see page 187)

SERVES SIX

Banana parfait with chocolate sauce

Bananas are not just cyclists' food. A great source of protein when I'm out on my mountain bike, but not always taken seriously in the kitchen. Hopefully, this will redress the balance. The lemon juice is important as it heightens the banana flavour and prevents it all from becoming too rich. This is cooking for taste, not stodge.

6 ripe bananas, peeled and chopped
Juice and finely grated zest of 1 lemon
75 ml (3 fl oz) dark rum
12 egg yolks
225 g (8 oz) caster sugar
600 ml (1 pint) double cream

FOR THE CHOCOLATE SAUCE:

225 g (8 oz) good-quality plain chocolate (65% cocoa solids), grated
85 ml (3 fl oz) milk

SERVES TWELVE

For the parfait, lightly oil a 1.2 litre (2 pint) terrine dish and line with a large sheet of clingfilm, leaving a good overhang.

Purée the bananas, lemon juice and zest and rum in a food processor until smooth. Put the egg yolks and sugar into a large mixing bowl and rest it over a pan of barely simmering water, making sure the water isn't touching the base of the bowl. Whisk until the mixture has increased in volume and is thick enough to leave a trail on the surface for a few seconds when drizzled from the whisk. Remove the bowl from the pan and whisk in the banana purée.

Whip the cream to soft peaks and very gently fold it into the banana mixture. Pour it into the prepared terrine dish and cover loosely with the overhanging clingfilm. Freeze for at least 6 hours, until firm.

For the chocolate sauce, put the chocolate and milk into a small bowl and rest it over a pan of barely simmering water. Leave until melted and then give it a quick blitz with a hand blender. Serve warm.

To serve, unmould the banana parfait onto a board and peel off the clingfilm. Dip a large knife into warm water, dry quickly on a cloth and then use to cut the parfait into slices about 1 cm (½ in) thick. Place a slice of the parfait on each plate and serve drizzled with the chocolate sauce.

Cherry and Almond Tart

This has been one of our most successful puddings at the restaurant. But don't make the mistake I made during the filming of *Wild Harvest*, when I mistook a bowl of salt for caster sugar. The tart should be eaten warm, when the pastry will still be crumbly and light. Brambles or other soft fruit could be substituted for the cherries. Serve with cold *crème anglaise* (otherwise known as custard!), to evoke memories of childhood puddings, or with Cinnamon Ice-cream (see page 135).

- 1 quantity Sweet Flan Pastry (see page 186)
- 250 g (9 oz) softened unsalted butter
- 250 g (9 oz) caster sugar
- 25 g (1 oz) plain flour
- 250 g (9 oz) ground almonds
- 4 medium eggs
- 600 g (18 oz) can of pitted black cherries, drained
- 3 tablespoons apricot jam

SERVES EIGHT TO TEN

Use the pastry to line a 25 cm (10 in) flan ring and bake blind as instructed on page 186.

Reduce the oven to 160°C/325°F/Gas Mark 3.

Cream the butter and sugar together in a large mixing bowl until very pale and thick. Beat in the flour and a quarter of the ground almonds until smooth, then beat in the eggs, one a time. Fold in the remaining ground almonds. (You can successfully freeze the mixture at this stage if you wish.)

Spread the almond frangipane mixture in the flan case and then dot the cherries here and there over the top. Protect the edges of the pastry with very thin strips of foil and bake the tart for 1 hour or until risen and golden.

Put the apricot jam into a small pan and leave to melt over a low heat. Add a little water if it is very thick. Press it through a sieve to remove any lumps and then brush it liberally over the top of the tart to glaze. Serve warm, with Crème Anglaise (see page 164) or Cinnamon Ice-cream (see page 135).

OVERLEAF:
Cherry and Almond Tart
(see above)

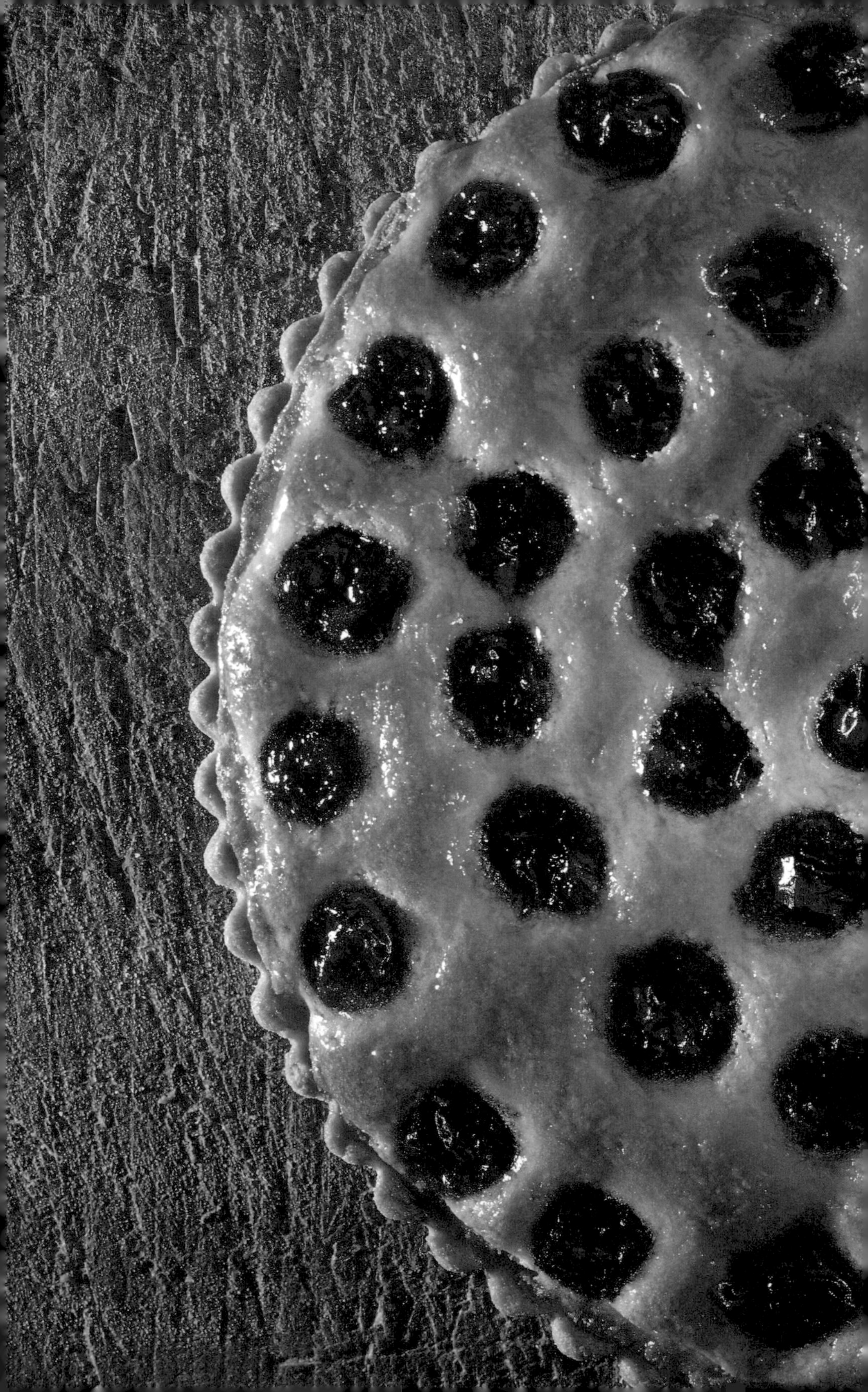

Banana Crêpes with Rum Cream

I don't need an excuse to make a feast of bananas and I defy you to eat many of these without needing a nap, or a wheelchair to ferry you from the table. They're far from sensible, but that's what puddings are for. Partner them with an Australian Liqueur Muscat to compound the effect.

50 g (2 oz) butter
8 ripe bananas, cut into slices on the diagonal
4 tablespoons dark soft brown sugar or dark muscovado sugar
1 tablespoon lemon juice

FOR THE CRÊPE BATTER:

2 medium eggs
20 g (3/4 oz) caster sugar
250 ml (8 fl oz) milk
90 g (3 1/2 oz) plain flour
20 g (3/4 oz) Clarified Butter (see page 184), melted, plus extra for cooking the crêpes

FOR THE RUM CREAM:

2 tablespoons dark soft brown sugar or dark muscovado sugar
50 ml (2 fl oz) dark rum
1 ripe banana, chopped
300 ml (10 fl oz) double cream

SERVES EIGHT

To make the crêpe batter, break the eggs into a bowl and whisk in the sugar and half the milk. Whisk in the flour and the melted clarified butter until smooth, then gradually whisk in the remaining milk. Set aside and leave to rest for 1 hour.

Heat a 15–18 cm (6–7 in) crêpe pan until hot. Brush with a little clarified butter, pour in some of the batter (about 2 tablespoons) and tilt the pan until the mixture covers the base in a thin, even layer – as soon as you have cooked a couple you will be able to judge how much you will need for the rest. Cook over a high heat for 1–2 minutes, until golden underneath, then lift up the edge with a palette knife, flip it over and cook for 30 seconds–1 minute longer, until lightly browned. Tip out onto a plate and continue like this, layering the crêpes up with squares of greaseproof paper, until you have made about 16. The pancakes can be made in advance and even frozen, layered with greaseproof paper.

For the rum cream, put the sugar and rum into a small pan and bring to the boil, stirring. Add the chopped banana and simmer for 5 minutes, until the mixture has reduced and thickened. Now stir in the double cream and bring the mixture back to the boil. Blitz briefly with a hand-held blender until smooth, or pass through a fine sieve, then return to the pan and keep warm.

Pre-heat the oven to 180°C/350°F/Gas Mark 4.

To serve, put the crêpes on a heatproof plate, cover with foil and heat through in the oven (or cover with clingfilm and microwave) until hot. Melt the butter in a large frying pan (or 2 smaller ones), add the banana slices in a single layer and fry over a high heat for 1–2 minutes on each side, until lightly browned. Sprinkle with the sugar and lemon juice and remove from the heat. Spoon a few of the bananas onto a quarter of each crêpe. Fold the crêpes in half and then in half once more to make cone-shaped parcels. Place 2 pancakes in each serving bowl, spoon over the rum cream and serve immediately.

MINCEMEAT TART WITH CRÉME FRAÎCHE

You don't need to wait until Christmas to enjoy this. The filling is made by adding a few extra ingredients to a standard jar of mincemeat. Do look for good quality, ready-to-eat dried fruit, so you'll have a rich moist filling.

- 225 g (8 oz) luxury mixed dried fruit, such as figs, prunes, dates, apricots and raisins
- 400 g (14 oz) jar of mincemeat
- Juice and finely grated zest of 1 orange
- 1 Granny Smith apple, peeled, cored and grated
- 25 g (1 oz) sugar
- 50 ml (2 fl oz) dark rum
- 2 quantities of Sweet Flan Pastry (see page 186)
- Caster sugar for dusting
- Crème fraîche, to serve

SERVES EIGHT

Chop the dried fruits into raisin-sized pieces and then stir them into the mincemeat with the orange juice and zest, grated apple, sugar and rum. If possible, cover and leave for 2–3 days to allow the mixture to absorb the orange juice and rum.

Pre heat the oven to 200°C/400°F/Gas Mark 6.

Roll out half the pastry on a lightly floured work surface and use to line a 25 cm (10 in) loose-bottomed metal flan tin. Spoon in the mincemeat mixture and lightly level the top. Roll out the remaining pastry to a round about 28 cm (11 in) in diameter. Brush the edge of the pastry case with a little water, lay the remaining pastry on top and press the edges together well to seal. Trim away the excess pastry. Prick the top here and there with a fork and bake for 30–35 minutes, or until pale golden. Remove from the oven, dust with caster sugar and cut into wedges. Serve warm, with crème fraîche scooped with an ice-cream scoop.

VARIATION

You could use the pastry to line individual tartlet tins instead and bake them for 10–15 minutes.

OVERLEAF:
Mincemeat Tart with Créme Fraîche (see above)

Panettone and Butter Pudding

Panettone, a rich Italian fruit bread often served as a Christmas treat, gives a classic pudding a new lease of life. Trawl your local delicatessen for a January bargain. It doesn't matter if it's a little stale as the bread will be softened by the cream. However, it shouldn't be in any way heavy or eggy. Panettone has enough fruit for my taste, but you could add some raisins that have been soaked in rum or Calvados.

225 g (8 oz) butter, melted
1 vanilla pod
300 ml (10 fl oz) double cream
300 ml (10 fl oz) milk
6 medium egg yolks
50 g (2 oz) caster sugar
500 g (1 lb) panettone, cut into slices 1 cm (1/2 in) thick
2 tablespoons light soft brown sugar

FOR THE CRÈME ANGLAISE:
600 ml (1 pint) milk
6 egg yolks
65 g (2 1/2 oz) caster sugar

SERVES EIGHT

Pre-heat the oven to 150°C/300°F/Gas Mark 2. Grease a 900 g (2 lb) loaf tin with some of the melted butter.

Split open the vanilla pod, scrape out the seeds and put both the seeds and the pod into a pan with the double cream and milk. Bring the mixture slowly to the boil, then remove from the heat and leave to infuse for 20 minutes. Whisk the egg yolks and caster sugar together in a bowl until pale and creamy. Reheat the cream and milk, then lift the vanilla pod out of the pan and set aside for making the crème anglaise. Whisk the hot cream and milk into the egg yolks. Return the mixture to the pan and cook over a gentle heat, stirring constantly, until it thickens enough to coat the back of the wooden spoon lightly.

Now cut the panettone slices into pieces that will fit snugly into the tin. Place one layer of panettone in the tin and pour over a third of the melted butter. Leave for a few seconds to allow it to seep into the bread and then pour over a third of the custard. Repeat this twice more and then cover with the remaining slices of panettone and sprinkle them with the brown sugar.

Place the tin in a small roasting tin and pour in enough boiling water to come half way up the sides of the loaf tin. Carefully slide it into the oven and bake for 45 minutes–1 hour, until just set (test it with a skewer).

Meanwhile, for the crème anglaise, put the milk and the reserved vanilla pod into a pan and bring to the boil. Remove from the heat and leave to infuse for

20 minutes. Whisk the egg yolks and sugar together until pale and creamy. Lift out the vanilla pod and whisk the hot milk into the yolks. Return to the pan and cook over a gentle heat, stirring constantly, until it thickens enough to coat the back of the wooden spoon lightly. Set aside and keep warm.

Remove the pudding from the oven, lift out of the water and set aside to cool slightly. Slice and serve on warmed plates, surrounded by the warm crème anglaise.

LEMON AND SUGAR CRÊPES

Lemons are a dream. You could eat them in every dish in a five-course meal and never know you'd had the same thing more than once. Nor do they have to be fancy to be delicious. I remember my mum making these. The lemon and sugar combine to make a lovely syrup, which in turn soaks into the pancakes.

- 1 quantity of crêpes (see page 160)
- 3–4 lemons (depending on how juicy they are)
- About 6 tablespoons caster sugar

SERVES FOUR

Squeeze the juice out of 2 or 3 of the lemons. Cut the remaining lemon into 8 wedges. Then simply heat the crêpes through in the oven or microwave (see page 160). Sprinkle them with plenty of lemon juice and caster sugar, fold into cones or roll up and place on 4 warm serving plates. Serve quickly while still warm, together with the lemon wedges.

Plum Clafoutis

Clafoutis is like a sweet toad-in-the-hole and is a traditional vehicle for cherries. It makes a nice late-summer pudding when the sweet Victoria plums are at their best. It keeps well and can be reheated in the microwave. Irresistible with a scoop of Cinnamon Ice-cream (see page 135), you'll find it worth a detour from any diet.

- 75 g (3 oz) butter
- 10 ripe Victoria plums, halved and stoned
- 8 medium eggs
- 225 g (8 oz) caster sugar, plus extra to serve
- 1/2 teaspoon salt
- 2 tablespoons dark rum
- 400 ml (14 fl oz) milk
- 225 g (8 oz) plain flour

SERVES EIGHT

Pre-heat the oven to 200°C/400°F/Gas Mark 6.

Use 25 g (1 oz) of the butter to grease a round, shallow 28 cm (11 in) ovenproof baking dish. Place the plums in the dish cut-side down. Melt the rest of the butter in a small pan.

Break the eggs into a large mixing bowl and add the sugar, salt, rum and milk. Whisk together and then gradually whisk in the flour and the melted butter. Pour the mixture through a sieve into the baking dish and bake for 40 minutes, until well risen and golden brown. Dredge with caster sugar and serve immediately.

PART TEN

BASIC RECIPES

STOCK – AN INTRODUCTION

Good fish and chicken stock should have a slightly jellied consistency.

When cutting garlic for stock, always cut whole garlic heads across their 'equators'. This gives you solely the sweet garlic flavours and not the harsh garlic oil.

In the summer, it's best to freeze fish or meat stock immediately but in the winter it will keep for up to 48 hours in the fridge. You can make bigger batches by multiplying the ingredients up to any number, depending on the largest stock pot you have. I find that the bigger the batch the better the stock.

Nage (Marinated Vegetable Stock)

This stock is essential to the making of Nage Butter Sauce, which crops up regularly throughout this book, so make big batches of this when you can. It freezes well and the ingredients are always reasonably easy to get. Freeze it in 600 ml (1 pint) tubs, and defrost when you need it.

1 large onion
1 leek
2 sticks of celery
1 fennel bulb (optional)
4 large carrots
1 head of garlic, sliced in half across its equator
8 white peppercorns, crushed
1 teaspoon pink peppercorns
1 teaspoon coriander seeds
1 star anise
1 bay leaf
40 g (1 1/2 oz) mixed fresh herbs
300 ml (10 fl oz) white wine

MAKES 1.2 LITRES (2 PINTS)

Chop all of the vegetables into 1 cm (1/2 in) dice, place in a pot and cover with water. Add the garlic, peppercorns, coriander seeds, star anise and bay leaf, bring to the boil and simmer for 8 minutes. Add the fresh herbs and simmer for a further 3 minutes. Now add the white wine and remove from the heat. Leave covered and allow to marinate for 48 hours in a cool place.

Once marinated, strain the stock through a fine sieve. It can be used immediately or frozen for up to 6 weeks.

Fish stock

750 g (1 ½ lb) fish bones, preferably sole, turbot or brill
1.2 litres (2 pints) cold water
½ medium-sized onion, finely diced
1 white of leek, finely diced
1 celery stick, finely diced
6 white peppercorns
½ bay leaf
15 g (½ oz) fresh herbs; try chevil, parsley, tarragon and coriander
1 tablespoon olive oil
300 ml (10 fl oz) dry white wine

MAKES ABOUT 300 ML (10 FL OZ)

Soak the fish bones in cold water for half an hour. Drain, wash and roughly chop.

In a medium-sized saucepan, gently sweat all of the finely diced vegetables, peppercorns, bay leaf and herbs in the olive oil until soft, but without colouring them. Add the white wine and boil until nearly dry. Now add the fish bones and stir to coat. Pour over enough cold water just to cover the mixture (about 1.2 litres/2 pints). Bring it to the boil, skim, and then simmer for about 18 minutes (do *not* allow it to boil). Remove it from the heat and allow to stand until cool (this takes about 3–4 hours).

Once cooled, pour the stock through a sieve or colander, then pass it through a fine sieve into a tall container. Place in the fridge and leave it overnight to allow it to settle.

The next day, skim off any scum that has settled on the top, then spoon off all the clear jellied stock, which should then be frozen until needed.

You may notice some white gunge at the bottom of the container – urg. This should not be considered edible and should be disposed of in a humane fashion.

Chicken stock

- 3 chicken carcasses, skin and fat removed
- 1 large carrot, quartered
- 2 medium leeks
- 2 celery sticks, halved lengthwise
- 1 onion with skin left on, quartered
- 1 small head of garlic, halved across its equator
- 6 white peppercorns
- 1 bay leaf
- 1 sprig of thyme
- 15 g (1/2 oz) parsley or tarragon stalks

MAKES 1.25 LITRES (2 1/4 PINTS)

Place the carcasses in a pot large enough for the bones to take up half its depth. *Just* cover them with about 2.25 litres (4 pints) of cold water (too much water and you'll end up diluting it) and bring to the boil.

Once boiling, skim off the fat and any scum from the surface. Add the rest of the ingredients, all of which should lie on top of the carcasses. Adjust the heat to a simmer and skim once more.

The simmering stock will now rise and fall through the vegetables, which act as a filter, absorbing all of the gunk from the liquid and leaving it crystal clear.

Leave it to simmer like this for 3–4 hours, tasting regularly. You should eventually notice the point at which the flavour stops improving. This means it's ready.

Remove the pan from the heat and empty the stock into a colander set over a bowl. Now pass the stock through a fine sieve into a tall container or 2.5 litre (4 pint) jug. Cover it and allow it to cool by placing it in a sink of cold water.

When it's cool, place it in the fridge overnight so that any fat settles on top. Skim off the fat and spoon out the now jellied stock into tubs. Freeze until ready to use.

Beef stock

Making beef stock is messy and time consuming (it has to be simmered for 8 hours) and is only really necessary for 'jus' sauces – that is, those sauces which are just the reduction of a stock, needing the 'body' of a beef stock to prevent them becoming watery.

Usually, I just add a little cream and butter to my sauces to achieve this. Some sauces, however, really need a bit of beef stock.

- 4.5 kg (10 lb) beef knuckle bones
- 1 pig's trotter
- 900 g (2 lb) shin of beef
- 2 large carrots, cut into 2.5 cm (1 in) lengths
- 2 large onions, each cut into 8 wedges
- 2 large leeks, cut into 2.5 cm (1 in) lengths
- 2 celery sticks, cut into 2.5 cm (1 in) lengths
- 1 head of garlic, halved across its equator
- 15 g (1/2 oz) parsley or tarragon stalks
- 1 bay leaf
- 1 large sprig of thyme
- 12 whole black peppercorns
- 3 plum tomatoes, quartered
- 2 tablespoons tomato purée
- 300 ml (10 fl oz) red wine

MAKES 1.2 LITRES (2 PINTS)

Pre-heat the oven to 200°C/400°F/Gas Mark 6.

Place the beef knuckle bones in a large roasting tray. Put it into the hot oven for approximately 1 hour until the bones are well browned. Tip off the liquid marrow fat and reserve.

Heat a large stock pot until very hot and add 3 tablespoons of the marrow fat (which should smoke as soon as it hits the pan). Add all the vegetables (apart from the tomatoes), the herbs and peppercorns. Stir thoroughly on a high heat until well browned – it is important to achieve a good colour without burning.

When a good, dark colour has been achieved, add the tomatoes and tomato purée and stir frequently until the tomatoes are cooked to a pulp.

Add the wine and boil to reduce it until just dry. Now add the beef bones, the pig's trotter and the shin of beef and cover with cold water. Bring to the boil, skimming the surface all the time, then reduce the heat until the surface barely trembles. Allow everything to simmer for at least 8 hours or preferably overnight.

When you wake up, get into the kitchen to strain off the liquid. I tip the contents into a large colander set over another pot. Allow the stock to cool. Once cold, skim off any fat, pour the liquid through a fine sieve into tubs and freeze the stock until it's needed.

Nage butter sauce

This sauce is my favourite and the one I use most in my cooking. It is a delightful, fresh, buttery sauce on its own but with the addition of other ingredients (freshly chopped herbs, chilli, pesto, tomato, shellfish... you name it) it can become anything you desire.

It is easy to make, and the base ingredients are easily obtainable. The one item of equipment that is essential in the making of this sauce though, is a hand-held blender. Without one, it is difficult to obtain the light, smooth quality that makes it so versatile.

A word on 'splitting'. This is an emulsified sauce (a combination of fat and liquid), so if you don't give it sufficient heat and keep it moving, then it will split – you will end up with big globs of butter floating on the top – not dissimilar to a commercial salad dressing.

600 ml (1 pint) Nage (see page 168)
200 g (7 oz) unsalted butter, chilled and diced
1 teaspoon lemon juice
Maldon salt
Freshly ground white pepper

MAKES ABOUT 300 ML (10 FL OZ)

Pour the nage into a small, straight-sided saucepan, filling slightly more than half the pan. Place on a high heat and bring to the boil. Reduce down to roughly one-fifth of the original volume. (It turns dark and looks thick and sticky!)

Turn the heat to low and plop in all of the butter. Stick in your hand-held blender or put it in an electric mixer and give it a good old thrash about until all of the butter has been melted and the texture is light and frothy.

Add the lemon juice, salt and pepper, tasting as you season, and keep warm (but don't let it boil) until it's needed.

If you let this sauce go cold and it solidifies, you can bring it back again by melting the sauce. It will 'split' – the butter will float to the top. Now boil 85 ml (3 fl oz) of double cream in a small saucepan. When it's boiling, use the hand blender to whisk it and, at the same time, pour the hot split sauce into the saucepan in a steady stream. And hey presto, lovely light sauce.

Duck fat

Not so much a recipe as a technique. Duck fat is made from rendered duck skin (i.e. skin that has been boiled down until the fat is released). It's a bit of a hassle to prepare, but it does impart a unique flavour to whatever is cooked with it. There is no substitute for the taste, but Clarified Butter (see page 184) will do the job. There are two ways to get your duck fat: the first is to follow the directions below; the second is to buy it in a tin from a specialist delicatessen.

3 whole ducks
1 sprig of thyme
1 bay leaf
1 head of garlic, halved across its equator

MAKES ABOUT 300 ML (10 FL OZ)

Remove the duck breasts and legs (retain for cooking). Strip off the skin from the duck carcasses. *Voilà*, duck skin! Keep the carcasses for stock.

Place all the duck skin in a medium-sized saucepan and add the thyme, bay leaf and garlic. Pour over just enough cold water to cover, put the pan on to the stove and bring to the boil.

Reduce the heat to very low and leave for 2–3 hours, until all the water has boiled away and the fat has melted.

Strain the fat off through a fine sieve into a container and store in the fridge until needed.

This will keep for 6 weeks.

HOME-DRIED TOMATOES

These are a sweet and plump version of what usually comes in jars labelled 'Sun-dried Tomatoes' and which, in my opinion, look and taste like shoe leather. Forego the supermarket chains and make 'em yourself – it's worth it. But beware! It *is* important to obtain really good, ripe plum tomatoes – the little Dutch waterballs won't work!

Approximately 12 hours of oven time is involved in the making of these, so don't plan on using your oven for anything else today. Better still, you can do them overnight. It's worth it – they *are* a taste sensation.

12 large, ripe plum tomatoes
Maldon salt
Freshly ground white pepper
50 ml (2 fl oz) olive oil plus extra for preserving (approx 200 ml/7 fl oz for a 600 ml/1 pint Kilner jar)
1 sprig of basil or thyme
1 garlic clove, crushed
Olive oil

MAKES 24 HOME-DRIED TOMATOES

Pre-heat the oven to 110°C/225°F/Gas Mark 1/4.

Slice the tomatoes in half, through the growing eye at the top. Then remove the green eye. Lay the tomatoes on a baking sheet, cut-side up, and sprinkle lightly with crushed Maldon salt and 12 turns of pepper. Drizzle the olive oil over them.

Place the tomatoes in the oven (you may have to prop the oven door open slightly open to keep the temperature down). Leave for 8 hours.

When you return, the tomatoes should be reduced to half their original size but not browned. Turn them over and leave for a further 4 hours or until they are nice and firm.

Remove from the oven and leave until cool. Then place them in a Kilner jar, add the sprig of fresh basil, or thyme the crushed clove of garlic and then cover in olive oil. These ultra-tasty beauties can now be stored in your fridge for up to 3 weeks.

I realize that this take a fair bit of time to do, but it *is* worth it. The only way you'll find out is if you try it...

CHILLI OIL

WARNING! This stuff is mega, mega spicy and you'll have to take care not to get any in your eyes or other sensitive parts. Used sparingly, chilli oil imparts a wonderful glow to many dishes.

(SAFETY TIP – don't fry anything with it.)

225 g (8 oz) ripe, red chillies
1 litre (1 3/4 pints) sunflower oil

MAKES ABOUT 1 LITRE (1 3/4 PINTS)

Slice the chillies in half lengthwise and place in a saucepan. Pour on the oil, plonk the pan on your hob and bring to the boil. Simmer gently for 5 minutes, remove from the heat and allow to cool (this takes approximately 2 hours).

Once cooled, transfer the chillies and oil to a plastic tub with a lid and store in a cool place for 2–3 weeks. Then pour the oil through a sieve to remove the chillies before using it (or else your oil will just get too hot).

I usually keep the chilli oil in an old olive oil bottle, but remember to label it well. A skull and crossbones will suffice.

Herb oil

If you prize colour and fragrance in your meals, this is for you. You could try it with individual herbs instead of a mixture. Chive oil retains its grassy colours better than any other, while the aroma of basil oil is unmistakable and guaranteed to lift the mood. This has a fabulous colour and makes a good garnish.

40 g (1 1/2 oz) mixed fresh chives, parsley and tarragon
300 ml (10 fl oz) olive oil

MAKES ABOUT 300 ML (10 FL OZ)

Drop the herbs into a pan of heavily salted boiling water for 10 seconds. This fixes the chlorophyll and keeps them green, giving the oil a lovely rich colour. Drain and refresh under cold running water to stop the cooking process. Wring them dry in a clean tea towel or kitchen paper and then chop roughly. Put the herbs into a liquidiser with the oil and blitz for 1 minute. Pour into a fine sieve set over a bowl, leave to drain and then pour the oil into a sterilised bottle or jar. Seal and leave for a day. Then pour off the clear oil into another bottle or jar and refrigerate. It will then need decanting before use, just like wine, to get rid of the sediment at the bottom of the bottle. Use within a week.

Saffron oil

The pungent, sweet, musky aroma of saffron is as precious as gold. Don't worry if this oil seems a little extravagant; saffron is a potent spice and a little can work wonders. Saffron is traditionally added to bouillabaisse and paella, but this oil gives it a starring role of its own.

150 ml (5 fl oz) white wine
1/2 teaspoon saffron strands
300 ml (10 fl oz) olive oil

MAKES ABOUT 300 ML (10 FL OZ)

Put the wine and saffron in a small pan and boil rapidly until almost all the liquid has evaporated. Remove from the heat, add the olive oil, scrape the mixture into a liquidiser and blitz for 1 minute. Pour through a fine sieve into a sterilised bottle or jar and leave for 24 hours before using. Use within 2 weeks.

Shallot and Tarragon Butter

Flavoured butters are one of my secret weapons. They can be stirred into otherwise lacklustre sauces and stews at the last minute. Whip this one out of the freezer whenever you think a dish needs an extra touch of richness.

- 225 g (8 oz) butter, softened
- 100 g (4 oz) shallots, very finely chopped
- 25g (1 oz) fresh tarragon, finely chopped
- Lemon juice
- Maldon salt
- Freshly ground white pepper

MAKES ABOUT 350 G (12 OZ)

Always make this well in advance so that it has enough time to chill. Melt 25 g (1 oz) of the butter in a pan, add the chopped shallots and cook over a gentle heat for 5–6 minutes until very soft but not coloured. Leave to cool, then beat into the rest of the butter with the chopped tarragon and lemon juice and seasoning to taste. Spoon the mixture onto a sheet of clingfilm and shape into a roll 2.5 cm (1 in) thick. Wrap well in the clingfilm and chill in the fridge for a week or freeze for up to 2 months.

Balsamic Reduction

This intensifies the flavour of the vinegar and also makes it thick and syrupy so it looks great when drizzled onto a plate, especially along with oils. It is excellent drizzled over roasted vegetables, Parma ham, salad, rocket or anything Italian. When you're preparing this, make sure that the kitchen is well ventilated – the fumes make your eyes nip! Stay middle-of-the-road; don't use the best 10-year-old balsamic vinegar for this!

- 1 bottle balsamic vinegar

Bring the balsamic vinegar to the boil and simmer until reduced by half. Leave to cool. We store ours in small squeezy bottles for convenience.

Red onion marmalade

The natural sweetness of red onions gives this a mellower flavour than ordinary onions, plus they're not that much more expensive. The marmalade is great with cold meats, game, chicken livers and bacon. Or add a tablespoonful to a meat gravy to make a rich onion gravy.

- 85 ml (3 fl oz) olive oil
- 1.5 kg (3 lb) red onions, finely sliced
- 120 ml (4 fl oz) best-quality sherry vinegar or, even better, Cabernet Sauvignon vinegar
- 2 tablespoons crème de cassis
- Maldon salt
- Freshly ground white pepper

MAKES 500 G (1 LB 2 OZ)

Heat the oil in a large saucepan over a medium heat. Add the sliced onions, stir well to coat with the oil and then season. Cook slowly, uncovered, stirring from time to time. until the onions are very soft and the sugary juices have caramelised. This should take about 1–1½ hours and the onions should look thick, dark and sticky. Now add the vinegar and cassis and cook for another 10 minutes or so, until all the harsh vinegar has been boiled off and the marmalade has a glossy texture. Leave to cool and then store in a jar in the fridge. If you pour in a tablespoon of olive oil to seal the top it should keep for 6–8 weeks.

Vinaigrette

This is my version of the classic French salad dressing. It has evolved over the years into this present form – a bit of an 'everything but the kitchen sink' recipe, but well worth trying. After all, ten years of research and development must count for something.

- 1 tablespoon smooth Dijon mustard
- 100 ml (3½ fl oz) white wine vinegar
- 100 ml (3½ fl oz) balsamic vinegar
- 200 ml (7 fl oz) hazelnut oil
- 200 ml (7 fl oz) sunflower oil
- 200 ml (7 fl oz) olive oil
- 1 teaspoon Maldon salt
- Freshly ground white pepper
- 1 garlic clove, crushed

MAKES ABOUT 750 ML (1¼ PINTS)

Place all the ingredients in a liquidizer and blitz them for 60 seconds. Strain the result through a fine sieve into a jug, from which you can pour the vinaigrette into any container of your choosing. I keep mine in an old olive oil bottle, which means that I can give it a good shake before using. A well-rinsed-out detergent bottle is also good.

Tomatoes Concassées

Skinned, de-seeded and with the acidic water removed, these small sweet cubes of tomato can be used for sauces and salads. Like everything else, the success of even such a basic preparation depends on the use of the best-quality ingredients.

Ripe, plum tomatoes (minimum quantity – 1)

Remove the skins from the tomatoes. To do this, you can either:

a) Slit a wee cross at the bottom of the tomatoes with a sharp knife. Pop them into boiling water and leave for a minute before removing with a draining spoon. The skin should peel off easily.

Or (my preferred method):

b) Use a blowtorch. First, spear one of your tomatoes with the tip of a sharp knife. Light your blowtorch and apply the flame to the tomato skin, moving on as the skin blisters. Same effect as (a), but much more fun.

Once peeled, cut the tomatoes into quarters, scoop out the seeds and set aside, then cut the flesh into 5 mm (1/4 in) dice. That's it. Tomatoes Concassées. Best used immediately, but they will keep for a maximum of 24 hours. (Keep and freeze the tomato pulp, seeds and water, for use in stocks and sauces.)

PASTA DOUGH

Fresh pasta lifts your cooking into the gourmet class, so it's worth learning how to make it. Pasta dough is simple to make, although you will require a pasta machine.

150 g (5 oz) plain flour
1 medium egg
1 medium egg yolk

SERVES FOUR

Place the flour in a food processor and start giving it a whizz round. Add the whole egg and egg yolk and keep whizzing until the mixture resembles fine breadcrumbs (it shouldn't be dusty, nor should it be a big, gooey ball). This takes 2–3 minutes.

Tip out the dough and form into a ball shape. Knead it briskly for 1 minute. Wrap in clingfilm and place it in the fridge for 1 hour before using.

Now cut the dough into 2 pieces. For each piece, flatten with a rolling pin to 5 mm (¼ in) thickness. Fold over the dough and roll it out, refolding and rolling 7 times until you have a rectangular shape 7.5 × 18 cm (3 × 7 in). It is important to work the dough until it is nice and shiny, as this gives it the *al dente* texture.

With the pasta machine at its widest setting, pass the dough through the rollers. Repeat this process, decreasing the roller setting down grade by grade with each pass. For most uses, I take the pasta down to the penultimate setting.

Once the desired thickness is reached, pass the dough through a second time at the same setting, then allow it to dry for about 5 minutes. Hanging it is the best way to dry the pasta: at Braeval, I use a suspended broomhandle, but for smaller quantities, use the handle of a wooden spoon (the other end weighed down with a heavy book), being careful not to poke yourself in the eye with the handle.

For lasagne, cut the pasta dough into squares (or rounds, if you prefer). For fettuccine, pass the dough through the machine's big cutters. For tagliatelle, pass through the small cutters.

WORDS OF WARNING:

Do *not* add salt to the pasta dough. This only toughens it.

Do *not* add oil to the cooking water. It will *not* prevent sticking and is therefore a complete waste of oil.

Do *not* dredge the pasta in flour to prevent sticking, as the flour turns to glue when cooked and, ironically, causes the pasta to stick.

To cook the pasta, have a large pot of boiling, salted water ready. Drop in the pasta, stirring until it comes back to the boil again. Cook for 2½ minutes, then remove with a slotted spoon or spaghetti fork and cool in a bowl of cold water. Drain thoroughly and, if not using immediately, store in a tub for up to 12 hours before use. Once stored, the pasta will stick together. To unstick, add some water, swirl around and drain again.

Olive oil croûtons

These are terrific in soups or scattered over salads to give a crunchy texture. A word of caution however – *don't* be tempted to nibble at these. Once you start, you won't stop and you'll end up having to make more!

4 slices of bread
85 ml (3 fl oz) olive oil
1 garlic clove, lightly crushed
Maldon salt
Freshly ground white pepper

SERVES SIX TO TWELVE

Remove and discard the crusts from the bread. Cut the bread into 5 mm (1/4 in) squares.

Warm a frying pan through (but not too hot). Add the olive oil and crushed garlic. Allow to infuse on a low heat for about 5 minutes.

Drop the cubes of bread into the pan and fry gently, stirring from time to time with a wooden spoon. After 10–15 minutes the croûtons should be golden brown. Season with a pinch of salt and 3 turns of the pepper mill. Remove the croûtons from the pan and allow to drain on kitchen paper. Discard the garlic.

Keep warm until ready to use, or store in an airtight container for up to 24 hours.

Clarified butter

Clarified butter is just the oily part of butter, i.e. without the buttermilk, and is essential for frying potatoes, to give them a rich, buttery flavour. It can also be used in place of duck fat (see page 173). You could buy it ready prepared in Indian delicatessens (as *ghee*).

250 g (9 oz) unsalted butter

MAKES ABOUT 200 ML (7 FL OZ)

In a small saucepan, melt the butter on a low heat. Allow it to stand for a few minutes until all the oil rises to the top, then skim off the oil into a sealable plastic container. It will keep for 2 months. If you have a microwave, put the butter in a plastic jug and microwave on a high heat for 1 minute. If it is not completely melted, heat again for a further 30 seconds. Do not allow it to boil. Continue as above discarding the watery buttermilk.

Savoury flan pastry

The variety of fillings for savoury tarts are endless but the recipes in this book are some of my favourites. The principles of tart-making are the same in every case, just the ingredients vary. Individual tarts look great but take ages; it's much easier and every bit as tasty to make one large one and cut slices from it.The tart case can be baked blind, and the filling made a day in advance. Assemble the flan just before baking it.

175 g (6 oz) butter
225 g (8 oz) plain flour
1 teaspoon salt
1 medium egg, beaten

MAKES ENOUGH FOR ONE 25 CM (10 IN) FLAN

To make the pastry, rub the butter, flour and salt together in a mixing bowl until the mixture has the consistency of fine breadcrumbs. Then add the egg and bring it all together into a dough. Knead this lightly 3 or 4 times with floured hands. Cover in clingfilm and refrigerate for an hour before use.

Pre-heat the oven to 200°C/400°F/Gas Mark 6.

Roll the pastry out 3 mm (1/8 in) thick and use to line a greased 25 cm (10 in) metal flan tin, 3 cm (1 1/4 in) deep. Fill with greaseproof paper and baking beans and bake blind for 11 minutes. Remove the beans and paper and bake for another 8–9 minutes, until lightly golden.

SWEET FLAN PASTRY

There are a multitude of fillings you can use with this. Let your imagination run wild.

175 g (6 oz) unsalted butter
50 g (2 oz) caster sugar
A pinch of salt
250 g (9 oz) plain flour
1 medium egg yolk
1 tablespoon cold water

MAKES ENOUGH FOR ONE 25 CM (10 IN) FLAN

Cream the butter, sugar and salt at a medium speed in the bowl of a food mixer. When light and fluffy, add 50 g (2 oz) of flour. With the mixer on a lower speed, add the egg yolk and the remaining flour a tablespoon at a time. When the flour is fully incorporated, add the water and mix it for a further 15 seconds.

Remove the bowl from the mixer, tip out the dough on to a floured worktop and, with floured hands, gently knead the dough 3 or 4 times until it comes together. Wrap it in clingfilm and allow it to rest in the fridge for at least 3 hours before you roll it out.

Pre-heat the oven to 200°C/400°F/Gas Mark 6.

Take the sweet pastry from the fridge and place it on a floured worktop. Roll out until the pastry is about 3 mm (1/8 inch) thick. Cut it into a circular shape, slightly larger that the diameter of a 25 cm (10 in) loose-based flan ring.

Press the pastry down into the shape of the flan ring, folding the edges over the top of the ring, and place it on a baking sheet. Line the flan with clingfilm (you can use clingfilm in the oven for this) or, if you prefer, use foil or greaseproof paper and fill it with baking beans (I use dried peas or butterbeans).

Place it in the fridge and leave for 15 minutes before baking it in the oven for 11 minutes.

Take it from the oven, remove the clingfilm, foil or paper and the beans and then place it back in the oven. Bake it for a further 9 minutes until the pastry is lightly browned. Remove, neatly trim away the overhanging pastry and leave it to cool until required.

STOCK SYRUP

Used in desserts, this is a 50/50 mix of sugar and water. It keeps for 8 weeks in the fridge, so make it well in advance and you'll always have it handy. It's good for poaching fruit and can be flavoured with cinnamon, vanilla, lemon, orange – you name it!

1 kg (2 1/4 lb) granulated sugar
1 litre (1 3/4 pints) water

MAKES 1.25 LITRES (2 1/4 PINTS)

Put the sugar and water in a medium-size saucepan, place on a high heat and bring to the boil, stirring from time to time.

Simmer for 5 minutes before skimming off any impurities that may have risen to the surface.

Leave to cool.

And that, as they say, is that.

TUILE CONES

These are very easy to do and make ideal containers in which to serve ice-cream (see Caramel Mousse on page 149 or Caramel Ice-cream on page 153).

25 g (1 oz) caster sugar
25 g (1 oz) plain flour
1 medium egg white
25 g (1 oz) melted butter

MAKES 8–10 CONES

Preheat the oven to 180°C/350°F/Gas Mark 4.

Put the caster sugar, flour and egg white into a bowl and beat together to a smooth paste. Beat in the melted butter and then cover and chill in the fridge for 20 minutes.

To make the tuile cones, drop about 4 teaspoons of the mixture well apart onto a lightly greased non-stick baking tray. Spread the mixture very thinly into approximately 13 cm (5 in) circles. Bake for 6–8 minutes until lightly coloured in the centre with a rich golden edge. Remove from the oven and leave to cool for a few seconds. Then, working as quickly as you can, lift each one off the baking sheet with a palette knife and roll into a cone shape. Leave to cool and harden. Repeat with the rest of the circles to make about 8–10 cones. Any extra ones can be kept in the fridge for up to a week or can be frozen for up to 2 months.

INDEX

Page numbers in **bold** refer to illustrations